Boundless energy

Boundless
energy

52 brilliant ideas for recapturing
your bounce

Elisabeth Wilson

brilliantideas

CAREFUL NOW

If you try out even a few of the tips in this book you should find yourself feeling noticeably perkier and more energetic. However, do remember that the advice in here should not be considered a substitute for the help you can get from your GP. If you're planning on changing your diet, taking any supplements or remedies or starting a new exercise regime, good for you, but please check your plans out with a trained and accredited professional before going ahead.

Although all website addresses were checked before going to press, the World Wide Web is constantly being updated. This means that the publisher and author cannot guarantee the contents of any websites mentioned in the text.

First published in 2007 by
The Infinite Ideas Company Limited
36 St Giles
Oxford, OX1 3LD
United Kingdom
www.infideas.com

A CIP catalogue record for this book is available from the British Library

ISBN: 978-1-905940-08-0

Brand and product names are trademarks or registered trademarks of their respective owners.

Designed by Baseline Arts Ltd, Oxford
Typeset by Sparks, Oxford
Printed in India

Brilliant ideas

   If you're reading this, you want more energy. Before you start, it's a good idea to know
   whether that's going to be the equivalent of a stroll in the park, or a steep climb, uphill
   all the way.

   A quick quiz that seems deceptively simple, not to say kind of obvious. But don't sneer
   too soon. You might be amazed by your score. This will pinpoint in seconds energy drains
   that you haven't recognised yet – or are ignoring.

   Yes, yes. You've heard it all before. You are what you eat. But the truth is, very few of the
   people who complain of being tired *are* eating enough good-quality fuel to stay healthy,
   much less energetic.

   Do you feel tired a great deal of the time? Do you need a couple of cups of coffee to start
   functioning? Is the only time you feel energised when you're worried, nervy and tense?

   It takes five times as much energy to slouch as it does to stand straight. If you aren't
   standing properly, your body has to work harder.

Brilliant features

Each chapter of this book is designed to provide you with an inspirational idea that you can read quickly and put into practice straight away.

Throughout you'll find four features that will help you get right to the heart of the idea:

- *Here's an idea for you* ... Take it on board and give it a go – right here, right now. Get an idea of how well you're doing so far.

- *Try another idea* ... If this idea looks like a life-changer then there's no time to lose. *Try another idea* will point you straight to a related tip to enhance and expand on the first.

- *Defining idea* ... Words of wisdom from masters and mistresses of the art, plus some interesting hangers-on.

- *How did it go?* If at first you do succeed, try to hide your amazement. If, on the other hand, you don't, then this is where you'll find a Q and A that highlights common problems and how to get over them.

Introduction

Over 50% of the managers in this country are really, really tired according to the Chartered Management Institute – which isn't very reassuring for the balance of payments when you think about it.

But then, they are managers, laden with responsibilities, cares and whopping salaries. Of course they're tired. Except that it's not just the stressed-out high earners that are feeling the strain. One-third of ordinary Joes (34% to be precise) complain of low-grade, general fatigue. And presumably another sizeable chunk of us suffer from top-notch, high-level exhaustion. Wherever you look in the media, the statistics keep rolling in confirming one fact: we're exhausted.

Where has all the energy gone? Why are we so horribly deprived of joie de vivre? Insomnia is one answer – 42% of us say our biggest health worry is lack of sleep. Our 24/7 society must be playing a part. Not so long ago, I met a very intelligent, street-smart woman who was utterly exhausted, but hadn't made the connection between her insomnia and the fact she checked her emails every night at around 11.30 p.m. Which brings me to what I consider the main reason for our exhaustion: a pig-headed refusal to accept some self-evident facts. Namely: if we don't eat well, sleep well, exercise our bodies, take time to relax and spend time with people we love (as opposed to people we share desk space with) then we're not going to function well.

When I was a slip of a girl, you had a choice. You could be the party animal, giving it loads six nights a week. Or you could be the goody-two-shoes who got a brilliant degree and a top job. Now, young people want to do both. Which has got to go some way to explaining why there are more 20-somethings cracking up than ever before with, yes, you guessed it, exhaustion. And we haven't even got onto the 30- and 40-somethings desperately overachieving at work and as parents. Perfectionism – or 'wanting it all' – has become something of a modern disease. Then we're surprised that we're knackered.

This explains why this book is a bit different from most books on energy, which advise lots of lovely complementary therapies and detoxing as a cure for lack of energy. It may well work, but I don't know anyone who has done it, including myself. And I know lots and lots of exhausted people, and lots of them are therapists. And they don't do it either. The truth is, when you're really tired, you don't need anything else to add to the to-do list. Which is why every single idea in this book you can do yourself, off your own bat – today, if you like. Because, if your energy levels are low, I think the important thing is that you take control yourself, right away, not wait for someone else to fix the problem. Having said that, I do think there is a great deal to be said for seeing an acupuncturist, homeopath, naturopath or other form of energy healer *if you follow their advice*. But the most important thing is to realise that you'll have to make changes – and the only one who can do that is you.

Exercise – even a very little exercise – will help enormously. Most people believe that sleep is their problem, but if they exercised, they'd probably find they'd sleep better. Indeed, as you'll discover from reading on, the research proves it. However, if you were feeling a mite defensive a couple of paragraphs ago at the bit about perfectionism, take care. I'm still haunted by the workaholic friend of mine who, totally exhausted, decided she needed more exercise and started training for a marathon. She collapsed in the swimming pool doing laps and had to be rushed to hospital. Use your head. If you're physically active and physically exhausted, what you need are some of the ideas on relaxation, difficult though they will be for you.

You also need to eat well and sleep soundly.

And if you do all that and you're still tired, then you might have enough energy to start on the really difficult stuff. Your personality. Your psyche. Your life.

What do I mean? Well, do any of these resonate?

- How can I change my job/my relationship if I'm this tired?
- I know the way I deal with the kids isn't helping but I'm too tired to do it differently.
- I need to lose weight but I just can't get started – it's too much effort when I feel like this.
- I don't suppose drinking half a bottle of wine a night is helping my tiredness, but I'll never sleep without it.

Being tired by work, children and a difficult relationship is a lot easier sometimes than facing up to the fact that we're not very chuffed with what life's thrown at us so far. Allowing ourselves to become exhausted is a great self-sabotage tool. There are some ideas on that here, too.

But while you're mulling over that one, here are lots of clever little tricks to help re-energise your relationship, your bank-balance, your wardrobe, your working life – even your dinner parties – which experts have taught me over the years. They're easy, and they work fast, so you can start feeling more energetic right away. Hurrah.

1

What am I up against?

If you're reading this, you want more energy. Before you start, it's a good idea to know whether that's going to be the equivalent of a stroll in the park, or a steep climb, uphill all the way.

The following quiz is designed to help you work out whether you need a few tweaks to work the magic, or whether a major change of lifestyle may be called for ...

ENERGY CHECK-UP

1   A friend calls to say he's just been presented with a couple of tickets for a concert he knows you'd enjoy – tonight. What's your reaction?
    (a) Terrific.
    (b) There's resistance, but you'd probably go.
    (c) There's no way you could go. You'd need warning to prepare yourself for a night out.
2   How do you feel first thing in the morning?
    (a) Ready for the day ahead.
    (b) Sluggish until you have that first cup of tea or coffee.
    (c) Exhausted.

3   If your partner is obviously keen to have sex, your immediate reaction (even if you act differently) is:

(a) Ooh yes.

(b) Oh no.

(c) It's been so long they don't even suggest it any more.

4   Imagine you have an hour free to relax on the sofa. Would you …

(a) relish watching a favourite movie or reading a book?

(b) start reading or watching television but probably doze off?

(c) be asleep within two minutes?

5   Which of these situations best describes your life?

(a) Lack of energy doesn't stop me doing anything I really want to do.

(b) I have the energy for most of my life but there are some situations when I just can't muster the energy.

(c) Lack of energy significantly impacts on my life and it's poorer because of that.

6   Does the thought of a holiday right now …

(a) really appeal – you feel like seeing new places, meeting new people.

(b) feel like just what you need – you'd love a chance to relax and rest.

(c) not interest you at all – the thought of all the organisation and travel sounds more trouble than it's worth.

Score 1 for (a)s; 2 for (b)s; 3 for (c)s.

Here's an idea for you... **Want more energy right now? Sip half a teaspoonful of honey dissolved in hot water with a squeeze of lemon added. Honey will rev you up almost instantly and also appears to affect brain chemistry in a positive way – making you more cheerful. But like sugar, it gives you an instant rush of energy, and too much can lead to a subsequent 'slump'. The acidic lemon slows the rate at which the honey hits your bloodstream, meaning you get the benefits without the disadvantages.**

If you scored 6–8. Remind me why you're reading this? Seriously, you're managing your energy extremely well and seem to be able not just to cope with all that life throws at you but to positively enjoy the challenge. The only reason that I can see for why you might have started to read this is that, although you are feeling terrific right now, your energy levels fluctuate. In which case, you may benefit from finding out how to ensure a steady flow of energy.

Turn to IDEA 2, *The real reason you're so tired*, to find out what basic habits are needed to maintain life long energy.

Try another idea…

If you scored 9–14 or over. You are managing your energy levels well. You are probably rarely ill and pretty resilient when under stress. On the whole you are finding the energy reservoirs to cope with life's demands but you may have been put through a particularly tiring time. Alternatively, if you have been feeling like this for a while, there could be a long-term drain on your energy. You are probably using quick energy fixes to get you through; getting to the root and resolving long-term energy drains will benefit you even more.

If you scored 15–18. The worst thing about your situation is probably how unmotivated you are feeling about making *any* changes because you're so blooming tired. By now, you are probably thoroughly fed up with feeling exhausted, often ill and below par. You know you have to do something because things can't go on like this. Taking it one step at a time will allow you to build up your energy – and when you start to have just a little more energy, your motivation will return.

'It's no longer a question of staying healthy. It's a question of finding a sickness you like.'
JACKIE MASON, American comedian

Defining idea…

How did it go?

Q   You talk about energy as if it's money in the bank, a resource you build up. But isn't how much energy you've got a function of how much sleep you had the night before?

A   *Some people sleep for hours and wake unrefreshed. The Chinese model of energy (chi) is that we're all born with a set amount and that we use it up during our lifetime, a bit like a battery running down. Some of us have more than others, and with good living we can maintain it longer. That's not our Western model of course, but if you think of your energy as being a finite resource within you, which you can eke out with the right healthy habits, that's a helpful metaphor. You have to protect your energy – you can get away with squandering it for so long, but eventually you'll have to pay.*

Q   Sounds ominous. What does that mean?

A   *I have met dozens of people who have experienced a total absence of energy – zip – and in every case, there was a pattern when you looked at it, of neglecting several key areas of their self-care for a long time before they got ill. I think this is true for those of us who don't have such dramatic falling off of energy levels, but who are feeling generally rubbish. We will have been going great guns for a long time, ignoring subtle warnings and then we get confused when we feel bad and lethargic, because we're just doing what we always did and it worked before. In this case, you have to go back to basics and start building up good habits that give your body a break. Especially if you don't fancy dragging yourself around on a Zimmer when you're older, because without intervention things ain't going to get any better, and they might just get worse.*

2

The real reason you're so tired

A quick quiz that seems deceptively simple, not to say kind of obvious. But don't sneer too soon. You might be amazed by your score. This will pinpoint in seconds energy drains that you haven't recognised yet – or are ignoring.

This quiz doesn't test what you know you should do, but what you actually do.

Be ruthlessly honest. If you plan to exercise three times a week, but actually only get to the gym six times every two months, then you *don't* exercise three times a week, full stop.

1 Do you usually sleep for at least seven and half to eight hours each night?
2 Do you rarely wake during the night?
3 Do you eat three well-balanced meals a day at regular intervals?
4 Do you always eat breakfast?
5 Do you eat at least two portions of protein foods every day (meat, fish, eggs, dairy, pulses) as well as two portions of wholegrain carbohydrates (bread, pasta or porridge)?
6 Do you eat at least five fruit and vegetables a day?

7   Are you active, on the go for at least an hour or more a day?
8   Do you drink at least one-and-a-half litres of fluid a day, not counting very
     strong coffee, alcohol or energy drinks and keep your alcohol levels within
     recommended limits?
9   Do you feel content and happy with your lot?
10 Do you feel that you have a good work–life balance?

This quiz covers the basics of energy. Score 2 points for each yes, 0 for each no.

If you scored 16 or over. You're doing very well. If you feel really lethargic, it might be
worth having a chat with your doctor in case there's any underlying medical condition affecting your energy levels, especially if you answered 'no' to question 9. You
may have some level of depression. Or you may smoke. (Any and all changes you
make to give yourself more energy will be totally undermined by smoking because
it adversely affects every single element you need to address in order to be energetic.)

If you scored 10–14. Any single one of these habits can wreak havoc with your energy
levels. If you answered 'yes' to questions 1 or 2, your sleep patterns need work;
'yes' to 3–6, your diet doesn't sound as if it's
including the basis for providing energy; 'yes'
to 7 and you need to think about moving your
body more; 'yes' to 9 and 10 and the way you
live your life may need an overhaul, or you
may be depressed.

Here's an idea for you...

**The easiest change of all
that will help energy levels
is to drink more water. The
prestigious Mayo Clinic
in the US recommends
adequate hydration as one
of the keystones of boosting
energy. Drink a glass of water
every time you go to the loo
and with every meal.**

If you scored 8 or less. You may be sabotaging
yourself on several fronts. Every 'no' is an area
you can work at.

Most of us know the basics of what we should do to be healthy, and as a side effect, brimming over with energy. Few of us do it. That's just a fact. Sorry to be a bit of a pedantic bore, but there are no short cuts if you're not addressing the basics. These are:

Turn to IDEA 3, *How to eat*, to find out what good-quality fuel looks like.

Try another idea…

- eating enough good-quality food to provide your cells with energy and keep energy production strong and constant;
- sleeping enough to restore your body;
- drinking enough fluids to remain hydrated;
- exercising enough to keep your lungs and heart functioning healthily and pumping blood to your cells, where it supplies the nutrients you need; and
- stopping smoking.

Perhaps you used to do all this. Perhaps you're a mother who just hasn't time to eat properly or exercise, and suffering from sleep disruption; perhaps work has got frantic over the last six months and you're so stressed you can't be bothered to look after yourself; perhaps your job demands a lot of travel – if you travel a lot, it's well-nigh impossible to take care of the basics unless you put some good systems in place and stick to them until they're habits.

The good news is that there are lots of short cuts that will help you and easy ways to get the basics right.

'Often, by the time we're willing to take a real look at what's happening, there's already been considerable deterioration … but you can always improve on some level if you start to take responsibility for the illness and therefore for its cure.'
DR BRENDA DAVIES, consultant psychiatrist and healer

Defining idea…

7

**Q   How come I got a tiny score, but I don't feel that bad most of the
time?**

A   *Of course, lots of people will have a tiny score and feel terrific. They're
probably young. Last night I drank two glasses of wine and I feel liver-
ish, depressed and lethargic today. I used to drink two bottles a night and
bounce to my desk at 7 a.m. Life changes. Specifically, we change. Anyone
over 35 is going to find it increasingly difficult to maintain high energy
levels while living a life that doesn't support your body in any way. But hey,
we're only talking about supporting your body, not giving up everything
that makes life worth living (and yes, life is worth living without fags). The
good thing is that when you make one change, it makes it easier to follow
the others.*

**Q   OK, I've got some changes to make, but I'm pretty healthy and
that bit about the GP is worrying me. What could be wrong?**

A   *Lack of oxygen due to anaemia or thyroid disease, which causes sluggishness. Depression often causes tiredness. Chronic fatigue syndrome is
another separate condition – it is characterised by extreme tiredness that
is not relieved by sleep or rest, for at least six months and accompanied
by other symptoms such as aches, pain or immune disease. If fatigue lasts
longer than two weeks or is accompanied by other symptoms such as fever
or nausea, or drowsiness during the day, you should speak to your GP for
a complete check-up. But don't panic: if you can't answer a resounding
'yes' to each of these questions, concentrate on some lifestyle changes and
you'll almost certainly feel better.*

3

How to eat

Yes, yes. You've heard it all before. You are what you eat. But the truth is, very few of the people who complain of being tired are eating enough good-quality fuel to stay healthy, much less energetic.

There are usually reasons (let's be kind and not say excuses). We know what we should eat but ... life is so crazy, we've been ill, we've no time ...

Some energy-boosting ideas will help even if you continue ignoring the basics, but if you don't eat well past the age of twenty-five it's near impossible to achieve everything expected of you.

On the other hand, follow the basic rules below and you will almost certainly start to feel better. All foods are equal in one way. They are broken down for fuel, but your body can use some of that fuel more easily than others. The sources the body finds it easiest to access are: fruit, vegetables, wholegrain bread, pasta and rice, because these are easy to convert into glucose. Glucose combines with oxygen in the cells to become ATP (adenosine triphosphate), which is stored and used as needed. If this carries on normally all is well and we have enough energy; when it goes wrong, we are lacking in energy.

THREE WAYS THE ENERGY SUPPLY CAN BE DISRUPTED

- Energy production is powered by vitamins – in particular the B vitamins and coenzyme Q10. B vitamins are relatively easy to get in the diet, but our ability to take up coenzyme Q10 diminishes as we get older. These nutrients are also destroyed by alcohol or smoking.
- Without oxygen, the glucose can't be used by the cells. Poor respiration, poor circulation and damaged blood cells (anaemia) all affect our energy levels.
- Some carbohydrates are *too* effective at creating energy. Refined carbs such as pasta, white bread and doughnuts are converted so quickly that if the body's given a huge dose of them – and let's face it, that's how it often gets these foods – it gets a bit overexcited, panics, and stores the sugar – and these stores are what make us fat. Our bodies are really good at this because those whose ancestors weren't good at it didn't tend to make it through famine.

Here's an idea for you... **Keep a food diary to see how, what and when you eat ... and, most importantly, why. This pinpoints situations when you find it hard to stick to the 'rules' and other habits that might be sabotaging your energy levels.**

So how do you use this information?

Follow these rules. They are simple, but don't underestimate how difficult it is to change habits, especially when it comes to food. Take it one step at a time.

The best piece of advice on changing eating habits is one that numerous nutritionists have given me – don't think of *cutting out*; instead focus on *adding in*.

A SIX-WEEK PLAN TO TRANSFORM YOUR ENERGY LEVELS

Each week concentrate on adding in one habit. You can do them all at once but, if you find eating regularly and well difficult, take it one week at a time.

1 Eat breakfast. Every day. No excuses.
2 Eat lunch. Every day. No excuses.
3 Start snacking. Never go longer than three hours without eating. Regular healthy snacks mean you don't overeat at meal times. Since eating huge amounts at mealtimes can deplete your energy – about 10% of your daily energy intake

Turn to IDEA 42, *Supermarket savvy*, for more on energy superfoods.

Try another idea...

'It's difficult to change any behaviour that since childhood has spelled "love", whether it's clean socks or a regular pay check.'
BARBARA SHER author of *Wishcraft: how to get what you really want*
(I'd add food to the pay check and the socks: remember bad eating habits are often tied to emotions surrounding comfort and love)

Defining idea...

goes on digesting what you eat, and a big meal means you're doing it all at once – snacking is less stressful for your body. It also keeps your blood-sugar levels stable so you have a constant flow of energy throughout the day.

4   Add in energy-giving carbs. Eat a fist-sized portion of wholegrain carbohydrate at every meal because it supplies B vitamins and doesn't get broken down too fast; for instance, wholegrain pasta, brown rice, oats or wholemeal bread (around two slices); Wholegrain contains fibre and fibre slows down release of the sugars in carbohydrates into the bloodstream. This means a slow release of energy throughout the day.

5   Add in energy-giving protein. Eat a deck-of-cards-sized portion of protein at lunch – and if you really want to see a difference in your energy levels, have some at breakfast too. That means meat, fish, eggs (×2), cottage cheese, cheese, tofu.

6   Drink enough fluid – about one to two litres a day – not including alcohol or strongly caffeinated drinks.

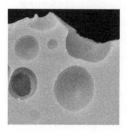

Q **My GP says tiredness is hardly ever caused by nutritional deficiency. Is she right?**

How did it go?

A *Your doctor is right in that it is hard to get so low on the B vitamins that you hit clinical deficiency. But we're not eating well enough – that's a fact. Government stats show that a huge swathe of the population is low on essential vitamins and minerals.*

I don't want to diss your doctor but, in one survey, around 75% of those who went to their GP complaining of tiredness didn't get any help. (One doctor put it as high as 90%.) GPs can help when your tiredness is due to a medical illness, but for most of us that's not the case. One more thing I'd add. What age is your GP? Around 35 to 40. Older? If so, she probably got about two hours of nutrition in her medical education where she learned how to spot scurvy. Technically, she's right but can there be any harm in supercharging your diet? Do you want to be 'right' or do you want to have energy? It's your call.

Q **This is all a bit vague. What do I actually eat?**

A *I've left that for you to decide. You will have to do a little planning. It has to be food that you like or you won't do it. Changing habits is very difficult. Changing what we eat is one of the hardest of the lot because it is so tied up with our emotions and sense of self. You know what healthy food is – pick some that you like. And remember that children need to be exposed to a new food up to twenty times before they like it – the same might be true for you.*

4

Why you need to move

Do you feel tired a great deal of the time? Do you need a couple of cups of coffee to start functioning? Is the only time you feel energised when you're worried, nervy and tense?

That's not normal. What is normal for your body is to move. Regular exercise gives you natural vim without having to resort to caffeine and adrenaline to get anything done.

Imagine an end to swinging between jitteriness and lethargy. Understanding how your body makes energy will help you understand why the need for movement is just that – a need, a necessity. Without it, you can't be energetic.

When you run for a bus, your heart beats faster and more blood rushes round your body. You need more oxygen, so your lungs start to work faster. The essential transfer of oxygen into your cells, and carbon dioxide from your cells, happens at a faster rate. Inside your cells, the mitochondria (energy factories) are producing ATP,

Here's an
idea for
you…

Apply the 'talk test'. The intensity that you're aiming for with cardiovascular exercise is such that you'd be able to hold a conversation with a friend while you exercised – but it wouldn't be easy. Make it your initial goal to exercise at this level for about ten minutes each session. When you get to the level where you could only blurt out one-word answers to a question, or you might collapse – you've gone too far.

your body's fuel (if your body is a car, ATP's the petrol). It's produced from glucose in the cells. This is anaerobic exercise. You can't work anaerobically for too long, because there is a limited amount of glucose, but the more you exercise anaerobically, the better your body gets at it (and the more likely you are to catch the bus). When we run out of glucose in the cells, our body starts exercising aerobically – producing ATP from stores of glycogen and glucose held in reserve in the fat cells of the body. And again, the more ATP you produce, the better your body gets at doing it. By exercising you train your body to be more efficient at producing energy when you need it.

What happens without that boost of oxygen to the cells? Without the stimulus to produce more ATP, our bodies become sluggish and lethargic. If we're not getting the boost from oxygen, we start relying on other things that raise our heart rate in order to get an energy surge to carry us through the day– notably stimulants like caffeine and nicotine.

Exercise's benefits to your body are legion, but when it comes to energy, it means you will have a constant flow of energy to achieve everything you need to achieve easily and calmly. Your dependence on artificial stimulants will diminish. Your concentration will also be more focused. According to a study in the journal *Medicine and Science in Sports and Exercise*, the physically fit scored highest on memory and intelligence tests and were more creative.

If you've never stuck to an exercise plan or found one that works for you, turn to IDEA 8, *How to start exercising when you don't really want to*. It tells you how to formulate a plan.

Try another idea…

But you know all this. What you may need is an attitude turnaround because the problem, research shows, is that we don't perceive exercise as a life-enhancer, but as yet another energy-sapper, draining yet more of our precious time. Exercise is one of the first things to go when we feel under pressure. In fact, it should be one of our priorities. When we're stressed, we produce adrenaline. Exercise burns it off, allowing us to calm down and deal with the pressure.

A THREE-STEP PLAN TO GET YOU MOVING

1   Every day – let your body out to play

Movement is play for your body. Every day give it a little of what it needs to be happy. It

'Exercise is the most effective anti-ageing pill ever discovered.'
    National Institute of Health, USA

Defining idea…

doesn't matter if walking up the stairs is as much as you can manage; walk up the stairs today. And tomorrow aim to walk up the stairs twice. Or go for a few stretches while you're watching TV. Or race your kids to the end of the street. Start small and build up the expectation that you will move every day – just as you would brush your teeth.

2   Every second day – feel your heart beating

Exercise that doesn't set your heart beating fast is still good for you but to start the energy-boosting process, you want to feel your heart beat, which means your lungs expand. This is cardiovascular exercise – and it includes walking, running, cycling, swimming and dancing. It doesn't include most forms of yoga, weight lifting or Pilates. If you are not used to exercise or have been run down, walking briskly for just five minutes a day is enough to aim for at first.

3   Keep going for six weeks

For most of us, with anything new, we will give up within three weeks. But if we can keep going for six weeks, we have the makings of a habit – something that, even if we slip for a while, we will return to because we like how it makes us feel. That's easier with a written plan of when and what you'll do. I urge you to keep it simple – start with just following steps 1 and 2 here for six weeks.

Q **I can't see it. How will walking up the stairs twice a day and going for a five-minute walk help get me more energy?**

How did it go?

A *Are you doing it at the moment? In order to have energy you have to move your body most days. Going to the gym once every two weeks doesn't work, if the rest of the time your greatest effort is walking from the front door to your car. This plan isn't difficult – that's the point. Just integrating the idea that you move your body every day, and every second day move it a little bit harder, is a great start.*

Q **I didn't think you had to exercise *every* day. But don't you have to do a bit more than just a 'few stretches in front of the TV?**

A *You're right. The current minimum guidelines for health are that you should include moderate activity for 30 minutes a day, five or six days a week. But we're talking about energy here, not necessarily optimum health. Personally, when my life gets very stressful, I can still find time every day for a little bit of movement. If I feel I am giving my body a gift each and every day rather than doing this po-faced exercise thing, I find it easier to achieve. Of course, the beauty of it is that once you start to feel more energetic, you want to do more, and before you know it you are meeting Government guidelines effortlessly. And you realise how much better it makes you feel, so you prioritise it even when you're busy.*

5
Stand tall, breathe deep

It takes five times as much energy to slouch as it does to stand straight. If you aren't standing properly, your body has to work harder.

The very simplest step for boosting energy is to ensure your posture is tiptop. This ensures you are breathing well, which means oxygenation of the tissues is maximised.

But there's more to it than that – the effects of standing tall have a profoundly energising effect on our psyche. Once I interviewed a consultant radiologist whose speciality was osteoporosis – the thinning of the bones that, in extreme cases, causes a hump so that the sufferer has no choice but to stare downwards. He was almost moved to tears by his patients' fate. 'Can you imagine the indignity of living like that, face down, slumped forward, unable to meet anyone's eye?' he told me. 'The pain my patients go through is bad enough, but the effect on their spirits is worse.'

What amazes me is that so many of us (myself included) do that to ourselves willingly. Neuro-linguistic programming – a highly successful form of mind coaching – teaches that changing the body's posture improves mood immediately. Start with these simple changes and see if it doesn't improve your view in the world.

STANDING – GET NEUTRAL

Stand with your weight balanced equally between your two feet. Make your knees soft and pull yourself up gently through your thighs, your hips, your spine. Relax your shoulders and let them fall away from your ears.

Now check your pelvis' position. Place the heels of your hands on your hip bones and position your fingertips so they are pointed downwards towards your pubic bone. Now adjust your pelvic position so the heels of your hands are on the same plane as your fingers, with your fingertips neither in front of nor behind the heels of your hands. You may have to contract your abdominals so that your navel goes nearer to your spine.

SITTING – THE RULE OF 90

When you are sitting in a chair, as often as possible observe the rule of 90. This means that your back is at 90 degrees to your thighs thus preventing slumping or leaning forward. A lumbar cushion at the base of the back of the chair behind your coccyx is worth investing in if you work for a lot of the time in a seated position. Or roll up a towel and use this instead.

Here's an idea for you... **Ask a friend to snap a picture of you standing as normal from the side. Your ear, shoulders and knees should be aligned along a line. If they're not, your posture needs some work.**

Your calves should form a 90-degree angle with your thighs at the knee. You may have to use a stool to raise your feet.

SPINE STRETCHER

This is a great exercise for freeing up your spine when you have been forced to maintain the same position for too long. It also gives you the advantages of an 'inversion exercise' – blood flowing to the brain – which wakes you up.

Read IDEA 4, *Why you need to move*, for an explanation of why a good flow of oxygen is essential for energy.

Try another idea...

Stand against a wall with every bit of your spine against the wall. Now starting from the top, the neck, peel your spine off the wall, vertebra by vertebra. Move slowly breathing easily until your lumbar (lower) vertebrae are off the wall and you are hanging forward with your hands reaching towards the ground. Feel the pull of gravity in your spine as your head hangs downwards. Now slowly reposition your spine against the wall, moving upwards, with the lumbar spine reaching the wall first.

WALK THE PLANK

Good posture is easy when you have a strong band of muscles around your middle – like a corset, your back and stomach muscles hold your body upright. This exercise is called the plank and it's a favourite of personal trainers because it increases your 'core strength' – which is just what you need to stand tall, breathe deep and thus have more energy.

'I want to get old gracefully. I want to have good posture, I want to be healthy and be an example to my children.'

STING, singer

Defining idea...

- Lie face down on the floor with your hands next to your shoulders.
- Lift yourself onto your hands as if you were about to do a press up, and on your toes so that your back is straight. Your neck should form a line with your spine and your face look towards the floor.
- Pull in your stomach muscles. Your spine should be flat, resembling a plank.

23

Tough, isn't it? But if you can do it, you'll stand taller than ever. On your first attempt, if you can manage this properly for thirty seconds, you're doing well. Build up from there to a couple of minutes daily. And it helps to have a friend check out that you are doing it properly, i.e. your back is straight. Remember it's called the plank because that's what you should resemble: if your back sags, you could injure yourself.

How did it go?

Q   My stomach is big and this makes getting the neutral position difficult. What can I do?

A   *Plank it. Yes, I know it's a tough one, but master the plank exercise above and you'll strengthen that crucial band of muscles round your stomach, then everything will seem so much easier.*

Q   I just can't get the rule of 90 to work in my office chair. Am I doing something wrong?

A   *It can be difficult. I strongly recommend a 'kneeling chair', which is good for your back. You kneel, with your bottom supported on a platform. Your spine is unsupported – that's the bit that makes it good for you – you can't slouch. As someone who has spent her entire working life sitting, I can vouch that they help posture and reduce back and neck strain. Type 'kneeling chair' into your internet search engine and see what comes up. Your employers may be willing to buy one for you – most are very big on health and safety issues.*

6

How to get enough sleep

The answer's simple – make like a great big baby.

Welcome to the nanny state. This is where we come over all strict. But it's for your own good, you know ...

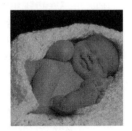

Lack of sleep is a growing problem, and like all health writers I've written thousands of words on the subject of getting a good night's sleep. I've interviewed most of the country's top sleep specialists. And what did I learn? That possibly treating yourself like a baby is the best thing you can do. Babies have to learn to go to sleep themselves. Most of us (but not all of us) learn this – but some of us (many of us) forget.

How much sleep is enough? The standard advice is that there is no 'right' or 'wrong' – it's what's right for you. So when people like Madonna say they can get by on four hours sleep, it's possible, but not desirable.

For the great majority of us who have normal working hours, aiming to get to bed by midnight and sleeping for at least six to seven hours is the bare minimum we need simply to restore our bodies after a hard day. Most of us would do better getting to bed significantly earlier and aiming for eight solid hours. Latest research is nudging towards nine hours a night as optimum. So if you're in the Madonna camp, thinking that you're doing pretty well on four or five, it's worth re-examining.

Here's an idea for you... **If you can't sleep, don't lie in bed for more than twenty minutes, becoming increasingly frustrated. Get up, read for twenty minutes, then try again. Don't put on a bright light, a TV or a computer. The idea is that you don't let your bed become associated with misery.**

Here are four lessons we can learn from babies:

BABIES NEED A LOT OF SLEEP

And so do most grown-ups, whether they like it or not.

Are you shaking your head and thinking you'd love to sleep more, if only you didn't keep waking in the middle of the night? Most people I know who can't sleep have tried everything that their pharmacist and doctor can suggest. Or they are self-medicating with alcohol. But that's doing nothing to deal with the original problem. Are you working long hours (and that includes housework)? Under huge mental strain? For the record, stress is the number one reason according to The American Psychological Association for short-term sleep problems such as frequent middle-of the-night waking and insomnia. If you know that something is keeping you awake at night, your only solution is to resolve the stress in some way.

BABIES ARE GOOD AT RECOGNISING WHAT'S KEEPING THEM AWAKE AND GETTING IT DEALT WITH SO THAT THEY CAN GET BACK TO SLEEP

Most grown ups aren't. But without resolving stress, and cutting the strain they're under, they'll never get enough sleep.

Then there are stimulants. Research shows that caffeine drunk before midday can still affect your sleep that evening. All of us, ideally, should be having our last cup by noon, and those who are sensitive should cut it out altogether or limit themselves to one cup of caffeine at breakfast. Alcohol knocks you out and then causes you to wake up in the early hours of the morning. Any sort of screen can knock you off your sleep pattern. I know one woman who was chronically sleep deprived for two years before she made the connection between checking her emails just before she went to bed and waking up worrying about work at 3 a.m.

For more on sleep, go to IDEA 50, *More energy with less sleep*.

Try another idea…

BABIES NEED A RESTFUL ROUTINE, LIKE A WARM BATH AND A BEDTIME STORY BEFORE BED

And grown-ups like a warm bath and a bedtime story before bed too. Grown-ups who are drinking, partying, emailing, watching TV, chatting with their mates on the phone or in other ways keeping their brains active could well get too stimulated to sleep. What they need is a relaxing ten minutes in the tub and a nice, quiet read.

BABIES SLEEP BEST IN A DARK ROOM

So do grown-ups. We evolved as a species to sleep in almost total darkness. Even a small amount of brightness can be strong enough to enter our retina even when our eyes are closed. This sends a signal to the brain that upsets the internal clock. Light in the hallway, shouldn't enter your room, turn the digital alarm clock to the wall, don't fall asleep with the TV on. Blackout curtains are recommended if your streetlights are bright.

'There are two types of people in this world: good and bad. The good sleep better, but the bad seem to enjoy the waking hours much more.'

WOODY ALLEN

Defining idea…

How did it go?

Q **Admit it, you've never had a sleepless night in your life. What do you know about it?**

A *Three or four – always when I was under a great deal of psychological stress – really, really worried. So yes, you're right, I don't really know what I'm talking about. Except, just as with nutrition, what I've observed is that the people who can't sleep rarely follow the above advice. They know what they should do and they get that mixed up with actually doing it. Or they know what they should do but I don't understand that their lives are just so busy, pressurised or important that they have to send emails or iron shirts at midnight. Which is, of course, their decision. But sticking to a routine works with a baby, often within a couple of days. Sticking to routine with an adult may take a few weeks, but it does work eventually.*

Q **I really do all of this, but I still am so tired the next day that I can't stop falling asleep.**

A *Do you snore? Obstructive Sleep Apnoea (OSA) affects 4% of middle-aged men and peaks at age fifty although it can affect anyone. Sleep is continually disrupted so that you begin to fall asleep during the day, or while driving. If you're overweight, smoke or drink alcohol in the evening, take tranquillisers or sleep on your back, changing these may help. If you snore heavily and are constantly feeling sleepy during the day, see your doctor: you might need to be treated by a specialist sleep clinic.*

Are you getting energy confused with adrenaline?

Lack of energy – are you kidding? Your problem is that everyone else doesn't have enough.

You're firing on all cylinders, dealing with crisis after crisis. You feel that you're in fifth gear while everyone else is pootling along in third. You feel, if anything, that you've got too much energy. You might be wrong.

What you've got is too much adrenaline. And that's why, despite the fact that you're coping, you have a sneaking suspicion that you're out of kilter. For one thing, there is your almost constant irritability, which doesn't turn you into a very nice person. So what's going on?

When life is busy you have to get really good at dealing with it. You make decisions at lightning speed, multi-tasking becomes second nature, you rip through tasks like a knife through butter. You're a lean, mean over-achieving machine. And just when you feel that you're right on top of your game, that's when life gets dangerous. That can be a sign that you're about to get ill. You're stressed almost permanently and using adrenaline to keep you going.

This quiz will help you work out if you're going into overdrive.

Here's an idea for you...

As a quick measure of where you are on the overdrive scale, count the number of times in one day when you feel everyone and everything is taking too long – from your spouse in the shower, to the newsagent counting change, to the red light turning green. Irritability with the rest of the world for going too slow is *the* classic symptom that your body is running on adrenaline. Any more than two occasions a day and you need to take action to slow down.

1   While you were eating breakfast this morning you were:
    (a) sitting at the table listening to the radio;
    (b) running around blow-drying your hair and finding your phone; or
    (c) breakfast is for wimps.
2   When you are deciding where to eat lunch, you choose:
    (a) the nicest place you can afford;
    (b) the nearest place to your desk: indeed, most often, your desk; or
    (c) lunch is for wimps.
3   What were you doing this time last week?
    (a) Give me a second, I can tell you.
    (b) It's a bit of a blur.
    (c) Why would I waste my time even thinking about it?

4   When you're forced to wait for a red light, a train or in a queue at the bank, you:
    (a) daydream happily;
    (b) get fidgety; or
    (c) start hyperventilating.
5   When you're watching a DVD movie, you're feeling:
    (a) absorbed in the drama – you use it to relax;
    (b) guilty – you should be doing something more productive;
    (c) driven to tears. Why do the characters talk so slowly? Couldn't the director get them to pick up the pace?
6   Do you find yourself finishing people's sentences?
    (a) Never – awfully rude.
    (b) Yes, when they are people you know well.
    (c) All the time. You've worked out what they're trying to say before they have.

If you scored mostly (a)s. You're safe from overdrive.

If you score mostly (b)s. Watch out for stress levels – they're on the rise.

If you score a mixture of (b)s and (c)s. You're running your life almost entirely on adrenaline.

If you scored mostly (c)s. The only thing you need to do fast is slow down.

Turn to IDEA 33, *Beware crash and burn*, for what to do when the energy runs out. *Try another idea...*

Defining idea...

'You can only live on adrenaline for so long; one thing's for sure, it doesn't pay the bills.'
  JOHN BARROW, American politician
  (Well, it does for a while, but not forever)

If you're running your life on adrenaline, becoming a 'stress junkie' in order to gee yourself enough to cope with your life, then burnout is inevitable unless you begin to find other ways of mustering energy. It also makes you difficult to live with.

SOME FIXES

- Clever people prone to overdrive exercise as a way of burning off their adrenaline. Be careful of becoming obsessive about it. You are pushing your body as it is. Overdoing exercise can hurt you further.
- The even cleverer ones give up caffeine and nicotine which stimulate adrenaline release, thus stressing their body out even more. Giving them up helps them recover.
- The cleverest of all slow down by taking time out every day, and time off every week, just for themselves. Meditation helps enormously, too.

Q   What do you mean dangerous?

A   In the last six months, have you noticed you seem more accident-prone? Have you cut up a driver who's annoyed you? Or purposefully driven slowly to antagonise some idiot who wants to overtake you? The main danger from overdrive is that you burn out. The secondary danger is that you go a little nuts and your irritability spills over into rage – road rage, queue rage, dog rage ... you'll get angry with anyone given half a chance – and that can get you into trouble.

Q   In my line of work, everyone's stressed. So what if I am too?

A   In the UK, according to one estimate, stress is implicated in 90% of all GP visits. Depression and anxiety are reaching epidemic proportions. 'Burn-out', the inevitable result of ignoring overdrive tendencies, is afflicting more people in their twenties than ever before, and that's a direct result of increasing pressure on young people and a more competitive and fast-changing world. We're supposed to respond to danger with the 'fight-or-flight response', but it seems many of us are experiencing danger from the moment we see our mobile flashing at us when we wake and know our boss is trying to get hold of us, to the moment we go to switch off our computer at night and see that nasty email from the Tokyo office which is going to wreck our day tomorrow. Everyone else in your line of work may be stressed. And everyone else may end up getting ill. All we're suggesting here is that you avoid this by swapping stress for 'real' energy that won't let you down.

How did it go?

33

8

How to start exercising when you really don't want to

Exercise is the one thing that will boost your energy levels faster than anything else. But what if you just can't get started?

Here is how to get started and stay started.

Research shows that when life gets busy, exercise is one of the first things to get bumped off the schedule. But before you berate yourself for your lack of sticking power, it's good to remember that, even for professionally fit people like personal trainers, exercise is cyclical. There will be times when it gets pushed to the sidelines. However, for those who have learned how much exercise helps them cope with a busy life, the gaps before they start exercising again are likely to be shorter than for your average Joe. If you've never exercised at all, this idea aims to get you to a stage where you too know that the benefits are so great, it isn't worth going without it for too long.

This idea is equally suitable for those who have never exercised regularly, and those who used to, but have lapsed. If it's too easy for you, ratchet up a gear, or jump some steps – but beware. Research has shown that there are two reasons that exercise programmes fail:

- we don't see the results we want (that's dealt with below); or
- we set our expectations too high.

It's far better to do a little and stick to it until you have the exercise habit than go nuts, join a gym, write an ambitious exercise programme and then give up completely after a couple of weeks of failure to keep to it.

DECIDE ON YOUR GOAL

If you've never exercised before, or haven't for a long time, please start with a modest goal. If it's ten minutes of activity a day – that's brilliant, as long as you are confident you will do it. Aim to visit your local pool once a week, then three times a week. Aim to swim once a week, and walk round the park once a week. Aim to do a yoga class on a Saturday morning.

Here's an idea for you... **When you're drawing up your plan, remember the acronym FIT: frequency, intensity, time per session. First work on frequency – aim to do some form of exercise five or six times a week. Then work on 'T' – the time you spend at it each time you do it. Then move on to the intensity – use hills to make you work harder, or go faster, or try a more difficult stroke if you're swimming.**

YOU GOTTA HAVE A PLAN

You need to make a schedule where every week you are aiming to do a little more, a little more frequently until you are exercising for around three to four hours a week – enough to get you out of breath for most of the time.

That could take a year, but don't think about that now. Stick your monthly schedule on the fridge. At first your goal should be just to stick to your weekly plan. Once you've got the hang of it, you can make your goal bigger, such as: run round the park, undertake your local fun run, cycle to the next town then cycle back.

Turn to IDEA 43, *Just a minute ...*, for more on how a little extra activity will up your energy levels.

Try another idea...

If you are very exhausted, very unfit, have been ill or are very overweight, all you might be able to manage is walking up the stairs. Fine. Make that your goal: to walk up stairs three times a week, then five times a week, and so on from there. Aim for cardiovascular exercise to begin with, that gets your heart beating, because that's the type that will give you energy fastest.

When I've not exercised for a while, here is my programme.

- *Week 1.* Walk slowly for five minutes, walk briskly for five minutes, walk slowly for five minutes. Aim to do that for three days a week.
- *Week 2.* Aim to do the same five times a week.
- *Week 3.* Walk slowly for ten minutes, walk briskly for ten minutes, walk slowly for ten minutes. Aim for four times a week.
- *Week 4.* Walk slowly for five minutes, walk briskly for twenty minutes, walk slowly for five minutes. Aim for five times a week.

Then I start running for blocks of time. Eventually, I'm running for most of the time and I'm doing it every second day.

'Exercise is labour without weariness.'
SAMUEL JOHNSON, English writer

Defining idea...

Q   I've tried all this, and it didn't work. So is that it?

A   *Then you need an exercise buddy. Research shows that those who plan to exercise with someone else usually stick to their plans much more easily than those who don't.*

Q   I'd like to lose some weight but this sort of programme won't do that, will it?

A   *Try to put the idea of losing weight out of your head. Studies have shown that those who exercise with the goal of losing weight are far more likely to give up. Why? Because you have to exercise really pretty hard to see weight loss – about six hours of running at a moderate pace every week. Concentrate instead on making it your goal to get more energy. You don't have to exercise anywhere near as hard to achieve this. You'll get results a lot sooner. When I start exercising again, specifically to feel better about myself and get more energy, I feel excellent in a week, and that's more incentive to keep going. Achieve energy and a habit and then you can think about cutting calories.*

9

Be effortlessly glamorous

**One way of saving energy is to stop wasting it.
Squandering energy on your appearance has to be right
up there on the list of activities to ditch.**

With a few changes of behaviour, you can
take a whole lot less effort with your
appearance and look better than ever before.

LIBERATE YOURSELF FROM CLOTHES-SHOPPING

This is the tip of a friend of mine who is a very glamorous editor of a major women's monthly magazine. She needs a killer wardrobe in her job but she is too busy to spend hours shopping either in stores or on the internet. So twice a year she devotes a weekend to it – and that's it.

I was once researching a book on time management and tested this as a technique for saving time. It worked, but I discovered how much shopping for clothes drains our energy – it made me realise how dispiriting it is dragging yourself round shops for the want of something else to do. How many hours do you spend drifting aim-

Here's an idea for you...

Linger over your lingerie – and we're not just talking to the ladies. All of us could benefit from taking a good, hard look at our smalls. Are they attractive, supportive, flattering? Underwear should be all of these things. Nice underwear gives your mood a fillip that's good for your energy levels. If you're a woman, get measured for a decent bra. It takes pounds and years off you (if you have a little too many of either). More to the point, it makes you stand tall, which is fabulous for your energy levels.

lessly around, trying on clothes that make you look frightful and damage your self-esteem? Now I like to wander round shops but I go for a mood-lift, with no intention of buying and in search of beauty (very energising!). I'll marvel at the iridescent pinks and blues on the eye-shadow display, sniff the fragrances, love the smell of the leather shoes, stroke the cashmere. (NB. I ask friends and family to give me vouchers for my favourite shops and spend them on my twice-yearly shop – so I don't even have to pay for it.)

Bonus points

You stop wasting money on 'mistakes'. 'Since I buy everything at the same time, my clothes really work together,' my friend says.

BOOK YOUR NEXT HAIR APPOINTMENT AS YOU'RE PAYING THE BILL

When your hair gets a bit out of control, it takes a lot more time and energy to keep it looking good. So why don't you book every six weeks? Because it's way down on the priority list usually. If it always takes you a few weeks

of 'bad hair days' to get round to making an appointment, schedule one for six to eight weeks in the future as you're standing at reception paying your bill.

Read IDEA 5, *Stand tall, breathe deep*, on posture. Nothing will look good if you slouch. Practically everything looks good if your posture is perfect.

Try another idea...

Bonus point

Your hair always looks good – and that's good for your confidence, which in turn is energising.

STOP CRAMMING YOUR WARDROBE

Every time you rifle through your wardrobe, think about those clothes you are putting aside. Probably the same ones every time. Have you worn them in the past year? Are you waiting for them to fit, or did you spend so much on them that you feel that you have to hold onto them even if you don't like them? Be strong and give

'*Why don't you get a hair cut? You look like a chrysanthemum.*'
PG WODEHOUSE

Defining idea...

away anything you haven't worn in the last year. The less you have, the less time you'll spend discarding things in the morning.

If your wardrobe *is* pared down to just what you like and what suits you, pack the winter ones away in the summer and vice versa. You'll find that when you have a loose, relaxed wardrobe, everything flows easily and you get less stressed.

Bonus point

Your clothes don't need re-ironing.

THINK ABOUT COLOUR CONTROL

Colour typing places each of us into a group, and each group has a whole swathe of colours that suit. You should stick to them like glue. There's something about this that smells a bit like fascism – after all, don't we know enough to pick out clothes that suit us? – but I've seen it transform at least two of my friends, who look heaps better since they started following the colourful way. Their clothes and make-up really flatter them, making them look better and younger. If you haven't ever felt you know what really suits you or your colouring is changing as you get older (hair and skin tones do) then a consultation might be well worth the money.

Bonus point

It saves loads of time, if you can breeze through a store discarding colours that aren't 'you'.

Q **I feel a bit defensive about this idea. Rubbish, I thought. But then all my clothes are black and frumpy and I feel listless most of the time. Is there a connection?**

How did it go?

A *If you don't care about how you impact on the world, terrific – discard this idea. But if you secretly yearn to change your image, try this idea. Go out and spend £200 on your appearance, or any other sum that is out of your comfort zone for spending on how you look. This is of no use for spendaholics, but is an excellent exercise for women who feel residual guilt about spending money on themselves. And guilt, as you'll discover, is a huge energy black hole. Spend £200 (or whatever) and you'll notice a subtle shift. You'll find you are being kinder to yourself in all sorts of ways including not feeling quite so guilty – and that's hugely energising. But perhaps seek some advice on clothes from a girlfriend or store adviser. Black only suits some people. It really is draining for the rest of us.*

Q **Can you tell me more about the colour thing?**

A *Type 'colour me beautiful' into your search engine. It is the best-known company in the UK. There will be a consultant near you and you can find out more on their website. They also produce a book to give you the basics at home.*

10

NAFH or naff?

That's Non Allergic Food Hypersensitivity to you and me – the new name for food intolerance. But many people swear that their once rock-bottom energy levels picked up after they sorted out a food intolerance.

But at the same time a whole lot of rubbish is talked about food intolerance, too. So how do you work out if avoiding a certain food might be the answer to your lethargy and irritability?

For a while, it seemed everyone I know was looking exhausted, fiddling with a lettuce leaf instead of eating dinner, and eschewing tomatoes because of their acidity. It is almost standard advice from alternative therapists to blame NAFH for the epidemic of ill-health and tiredness sweeping the country. Since one in four of us will at some time consult some form of alternative therapist, an awful lot of us are going to get the idea that we've got intolerances to certain foods.

Here's an idea for you...

Even if you don't have an intolerance, eating a more varied diet will boost your energy levels as it gives you a wider variety of nutrition. Substitute soya milk for dairy at one meal and rye bread, oats, porridge or brown rice for your usual pasta or bread. If you feel more energetic after such a meal, consider substituting more often.

But is it all a load of rubbish? Just another way of being 'funny' about food?

Conventional medicine does not have much truck with the notion. Your GP understands food allergy and that's a very different beast. With food allergy, you eat a food that you're allergic too – shellfish, peanuts, strawberries – and within minutes, you get very ill indeed. In fact, in the worst cases, if you're not pumped full of drugs, you could die. On the other hand, food intolerance is nothing like as dramatic. It's characterised by extreme tiredness. Symptoms might include diarrhoea and other chronic gut problems, migraines, headaches, rashes and bloating. The highest figure for NAFH is 45%; sceptical doctors say that figure is more likely about 5%. The trouble is, we don't know the exact mechanisms. The immune system is almost certainly involved but we don't have any reliable tests or cure.

Another sticking point for those sceptical of intolerances is that they are often to the most natural, pure foods. But this shouldn't be such a surprise. The truth is that nature isn't here for our benefit – it's here for its own. Cow's milk is meant to feed little cows. Plants don't want to be eaten which is why most taste vile and some are poisonous. Even those that are desirable to eat – fruits – simply use us as 'carriers' of their seeds but, just so we don't get in the way of their propagation, they have evolved to pass through our system very quickly (most fruits are mild laxatives).

So, intolerances are likely to be towards simple foods; they are also more likely to be towards foods we eat a lot. We are omnivores and can eat more or less anything. That's because back when we were hunter-gatherers, the picky eaters didn't tend to make it through

Read IDEA 32, *Get in the raw,* for more on raw food.

Try another idea…

the winter. Our species developed on a diet that was varied not to say disgusting. According to Allergy UK, the cause of intolerances is likely to be that we rely too much on one kind of food. Here in the UK we eat more wheat and milk, and that's what we're more intolerant to; in the States they are much more allergic to corn than here; in the East there have been cases of intolerance to rice.

THE EASIEST ANSWER? BOOST YOUR IMMUNITY

A decreased immunity in the gut affects the microflora of the gut. Food is less well absorbed, and the lining of the gut can become irritated. This becomes dysbiosis. This leads to food allergies and food intolerances. According to one commentator, dysbiosis is found in up to 85% of food intolerances.

Taking probiotics can boost the good bacteria in your gut and boost your immune system. (The Common Cold Centre recommends it as a way of guarding against colds.) Eat live natural yogurt or take a probiotic supplement such as acidophilus. You need to take a good quality product, however.

'Part of the secret of success in life is to eat what you like and let the food fight it out inside.'

MARK TWAIN

Defining idea…

Q I think I may have an intolerance and these measures didn't work. What next?

A *You can pay for tests, although their use is not universally accepted. A friend of mine whose opinion I respect has tried a company called York Test, and she says following their advice transformed her energy levels. Vega testing, where you hold a suspected food in your hand and have your electrical fields measured, is unscientific and I have never found it in the least useful.*

The only sure way of discovering if you are intolerant to a food is to eliminate it from your diet and see if you feel better. The 'gold standard' way is to give up all but the blandest foods – green vegetables, brown rice, organic lamb – for about three weeks. Then reintroduce foods one at a time, noting the effects that it has on your energy levels and wellbeing. It would be best to do this under the guidance of a nutritional therapist. The other way is to eliminate the foods that you suspect may be to blame.

Q I'm sure I'm intolerant to wheat, so why hasn't swapping to oats and rye helped.

A *Foods fall into families – if you're intolerant to one family member, you may be intolerant to others. Wheat, rye, barley and oats form one family. Potatoes, aubergines and tomatoes are another. Lettuce, chicory and arti-choke another. You may have to do some serious reading-up on the subject to sort out what you should avoid. Or, again, see a nutritional therapist.*

11

Finding work to make your heart sing

What do you do if your job is dragging you down?

It's really, really hard to feel energised when five days out of seven are dedicated to an activity that bores you stupid — or worse, saps your self-esteem. Yup, we're talking about work.

At any one time, 40 % of us are looking for a new job. If you're one of them, the chances are that your present job is sapping your strength.

Do you basically love your job but need to move on for promotion, more money or simply for a change? Then terrific. It's just a matter of time, sending out enough good quality CVs and brushing up on your interview technique.

Here's an idea for you…

Phone a friend – or three. You almost certainly know people who have transferred skills and started working in another career. Pick their brains on how they financed it, got their family onside, garnered the qualifications, coped with problems. Those who have pursued their happiness are going to have more practical advice, on coping with the good and bad, as well as more enthusiasm, than those who haven't taken a similar leap.

But this idea is for those people who know at heart that they are on the wrong track; that changing job may give a temporary fillip to their mood, offer new challenges and a change of environment, but really, deep down, it is going to be more of the same. You're the people who haven't yet found your dream job. You're the ones who fantasise about winning the lottery because it's the only way off the treadmill.

To find work that will energise, excite and stimulate you, you will have to do some soul-searching and perhaps face some hard decisions. Use the five words, often called 'the journalist's best friends', that are the start of any investigation – namely, when, what, why, how and where.

1   *When do you lose yourself?* Think back to the last time you were so completely engrossed in what you were doing that you didn't notice time passing. Were you painting a room, listening to your friend talk, dancing at a wedding, decorating a cake? Were you driving, shopping, helping your child with their homework, volunteering for your local charity? Write it down. Try to remember a few more occasions. It might help to remember what you used to love as a child. Did you love to wander about the garden examining flowers and rocks? Were you always at the swimming pool? Did you prefer to be alone, or hang out with friends? Search for your passion. Seek out your joy. Look at your list, and mull on it.

2   *What do you dream about?* Another version of step 1 is to think about what you'd do if you won the lottery and didn't have to work anymore. How would you choose to spend your time? Any clues there?

Turn to IDEA 34, *Are you getting enough?* on how to get more pleasure in your life while you look for a new job.

Try another idea…

3   *Why are you scared?* Ask why you're not fulfilling your dream. At the root of it will almost certainly be fear. That could be fear of telling your spouse you want to give up your lucrative job to become a windsurf instructor or it could be the fear that giving up a profession into which you've invested a lot of time makes you look a fool. The longer you've studied or worked at a profession, the harder it is to give it up. Think of it this way: you're not giving up, you're transferring skills; you're not wiping years off your CV, you are using past skills to find a parallel career that gives you satisfaction.

4   *How much value can you add?* It may take a while. In the meantime, try putting your most into the job you've got. Bringing a good attitude to work will almost certainly result in you doing well because most people simply don't – their work is mediocre – and that makes it easy to shine if you put in some effort. Being enthusiastic will energise you.

5   *Where are the soulmates?* Go back to your step 1 list. While you're looking, or retraining for your dream job, include more of what makes you happy in your life. Pursuing what makes you happy means you'll meet other people who share your interests, and who knows where that will take you? Listen to your instincts. While I was listening to a casual business acquaintance describe the re-training she wanted to pursue, the thought popped into my head: 'I should do that'. Two years later, I did.

'The brain is a wonderful organ. It starts working in the morning and doesn't stop until you get into the office.'
ROBERT FROST, poet

Defining idea…

How did it go?

Q   I trained for seven years and have worked for three in a job that doesn't satisfy me, but it's not as easy as 'walk away', is it?

A   *No, it's not easy. But it might save your life – literally, because that's your life going down the drain for something you're not sure about. You don't have to resign from your present job tomorrow; you just have to take it one step at a time. It might take a few years to get your support systems into place, so that you can leave and do something else. When I first began thinking about re-training as a psychotherapist, giving up my present job was an impossibility – I was supporting my family. A year and half later, because of circumstances I could never have predicted, leaving work was a possibility – and I was ready. Pinpoint what makes you feel good and try to incorporate those elements into your present job or, if you can't do that, into your life.*

Q   Isn't this all a bit vague?

A   *I don't know you, so I can't get personal. What I do know is that hating your job is a terrible drain on your energy. Passion is the only antidote. And following your passion can lead you towards a career that you never even thought of before. I know a lawyer who pursued his love of books by selling them second-hand at the weekends. Through his stall, he met another bibliophile. They started writing together, and fifteen years later, they have a successful film production company.*

   Another clue is what you hesitate to give up even when life gets frantic. If you always make your yoga class, what does that tell you about your passion? It was when I realised that, despite having a young family and a crushing workload, I had still managed to keep working as a charity volunteer, that it dawned on me that counselling was a passion for me.

12

Give your brain a break

Recharge your mind.

When your mind is sparking and sparkling, it's a lot more likely that you'll have the energy to achieve all you want.

Your mind and body are never more obviously linked than when it comes to energy. The tricks you need to keep your brain charged and ready to go (eating well, not overdoing booze) are the same that will pep up the rest of you. But you can save a lot of time by going directly to the mother ship and specifically taking care of your mind. The reward will be an instantaneous boost in creativity and better sleep, which will directly affect your energy levels.

To achieve this, we're going to take a two-pronged attack: livening up your mind, then giving it a lovely rest. And for best results, you should aim to do both every day.

Here's an idea for you...

Learn to speed-read. It's a useful skill that also improves mental alertness. Practise with a newspaper. Scan through the story to get an idea of content and context. Next, move your fingertip across the page underlining the words as you read. This anchors your eyes and frees you from having to repeat every word inside your head. Soon you'll be able to skip to every third line and eventually get the gist from just a few lines on any page. It works to make your brain patterns more alert and zippy.

GIVE YOUR BRAIN A WORK OUT

Aim to do this every morning.

Warm up

As soon as you wake, give yourself a gentle little challenge such as: counting down from 100 to 1; naming twenty capital cities or twenty girls' names beginning with P; multiplying the first two numbers you see.

Work out

Buy yourself a book of puzzles and set yourself one a day during the daily commute. Or do a crossword. Scientists now think that puzzles won't keep your brain from ageing, but will keep it sharp at solving problems and thinking laterally – and that's no bad thing. A little competitiveness is good for your IQ. Mensa (the British organisation for people with a high IQ: only those in the top 2% in the country can be members) recommends we do a puzzle every day, and observational science, even if not laboratory science, shows that there's a lot to be said for keeping the brain busy. Edinburgh University's studies of the so-called 'superyoung' – those deemed to be years younger than their chronological age by their peers – showed that the most significant factor they shared was an active mind open to new ideas and differing viewpoints: they read new material, listened to speech radio rather than watched TV (it takes more mental effort), and turned to the puzzle page in their newspaper rather than flicking over it.

GIVE YOUR BRAIN A REST

Research at the prestigious Tufts University
in the States discovered that people who sit
quietly for ten minutes a day, observing their
heart rate on a monitor and concentrating on lowering it, had reduced anxiety and
increased feeling of wellbeing and energy.

Four 'brain holidays'

Build these into your day as often as you remember. Aim for two minutes, building
up to ten.

- Try sitting quietly taking your pulse and concentrating on slowing it down (it
  doesn't matter if you don't; it's the concentration that counts).
- Take a look out of the window. Observe what you see but don't react to it.
  When you do react (for example, you can't help getting upset when you see
  someone drop litter outside your gate), notice your reaction and then let it float
  away like a cloud.
- The easiest meditation of all. Breathe. Just as normal, don't change a thing.
  Observe your breath. Notice how the air is cooler as it enters your nostrils and
  that it is warmer when you exhale. Feel the air reaching your lungs. Notice
  how your belly expands as you inhale, flattens as you exhale. When your mind
  wanders, notice it and bring it back to the
  breath.
- Light a candle, watch the flame. Concentrate on the flame and bring your mind
  back to it when it wanders off.

**Take a nap. Try IDEA 50, *More
energy with less sleep.***

Try another idea...

*'The basis of all well-being is
to learn to live in the here and
now.'*
DR JAMES RIPPE, American physician
and expert on relaxation

Defining idea...

How did it go? **Q** **What if I don't have time to stare out the window (and anyway, my boss would get upset)?**

A *Show her this. Taking a brain holiday makes you sharper and improves your productivity. Research on high-achievers shows that those who took a ten-minute break every two hours to shut their eyes and do some deep breathing, or looked out the window and let their brain switch off, did better than those who either didn't stop, or had a chat with a friend or watched TV.*

Q **I can't quieten my mind. How can I stop my mind wandering all over the place?**

A *Don't beat yourself up when your mind wanders. That's what minds do. There's no such thing as 'perfect' meditation. It doesn't matter how often your mind swings away. It is your intention to rest your brain that works the charm, not how well you concentrate. Simply bring your brain back no matter how many times you notice it drifting off, and know that it gets easier.*

13

Nuts to you

If your energy flags during the day. Or if you get food cravings that result in a crash-and-burn. Or if you simply – often – find you don't have time to eat ...

... grab your nuts.

Nuts provide a unique combination of protein (long-term energy release), fibre and healthy fats. They fill you up and keep blood-sugar levels stable. Keep a handful in your handbag or pocket and you'll find they keep you going right through to your next meal. They stop you craving fatty or sugary foods mid-morning or mid-afternoon – and that means you're less likely to pig out on sugary foods that give you a sugar rush followed by a slump. You'll also find it easier to make healthy, energy-boosting choices at mealtimes.

And there's more. Nuts contain the omega-3 fatty acids that are known to be so useful in maintaining a good mood, which will help you on days when you have no energy.

New research from Spain shows that just a few nuts a day could cut your heart attack risk by 30% thanks to the omega-3, -6 and -9 content in nuts' monounsaturated fats.

NUTS! WHAT'S NOT TO LOVE?

Well, their massive calorie count for one thing. Although good for you, these fats pack a hefty calorific punch but even their high-calorie content may not be as much

Here's an idea for you... **Buy yourself some nutcrackers and nuts still in their shell. It's cheaper than buying shelled nuts, it's strangely satisfying to shell your own nuts, and it slows down the rate at which you eat them.**

of a problem as previously thought. Another study found that people who ate around 50g of almonds a day (two large handfuls) didn't put on any weight over a six-month period. 'People who eat nuts eat less overall,' was the verdict of at least one scientist studying their benefits.

Start eating just a few nuts a day and your energy levels – and figure – may well benefit. Since each nut offers a different mix of nutrients, get a good mixture for maximum health benefits. All nuts will give you energy but by mixing and matching the types you eat, you'll maximise health benefits – more about that below. You probably don't want to eat more than 28g (1oz) a day in total in case you're overdoing it – but that's enough.

Walnuts

All nuts help the heart but walnuts are particularly beneficial because they are especially rich in alpha linolenic acid, which has blood-thinning and anti-clotting properties. Healthy serving = 14 halves.

Almonds

Almonds (with the skin on) are high in the healthy monounsaturated type (70%) and in calcium, which make them good for your bones. They are also rich in oleic acid – the ingredient that makes olive oil so good for your heart. Healthy serving = 20 nuts.

Brazil

Brazil nuts are chock-full of the antioxidants that fight cancer and heart disease, especially the mineral, selenium. Healthy serving = 2–3 a day. (28g of Brazil nuts is around seven nuts, but they are higher in the 'bad' saturated fats than the others so it's best to restrict these and mix with other nuts.)

Look at IDEA 32, *Get raw*, for a low-down on the benefits of eating raw food.

Try another idea…

Cashews

Cashews are a good food for your skin. They are rich in the fats, minerals and vitamin E that help promote collagen-formation in the skin, which provides a framework for healthy skin. Healthy serving = 16 nuts.

Macadamias

Macadamias provide a mix of nutrients that help improve memory and concentration. However, they are the richest in fat and, although good for you, have a high calorific content – so rich that they could upset digestion in sensitive souls who over indulge. Healthy serving = 8 (28g of macadamias is around ten to twelve).

Pistachios

Pistachios are one of the best for your heart. They help lower overall cholesterol and vitally, improve the balance between good and bad cholesterols. They are also the best nut source of the antioxidant beta-carotene and great for eyesight as they're rich in the nutrient lutein. Healthy serving = 20.

'**Women! Can't live with them ... pass the beer nuts.'**
NORM in *Cheers*, American comedy

Defining idea…

How did it go?

Q   Won't I get an allergy eating so many nuts?

A   *I'd hope not. But it's true that pregnant women are advised to stay away from nuts even if they don't have an allergy, in case their babies become sensitised. So, although nut allergy is something you're born with, this has to be your call. If you come from a family where allergy is rife, you may want to modify the above advice rather than get an allergy.*

Q   I'm guessing peanuts don't count, right?

A   *Peanuts, funnily, enough aren't strictly a nut. They are a legume, although very similar to a nut. They are good-value in many ways – full of vitamin B3 for instance – but you're right: any nut covered in salt isn't the best choice. However don't eschew them at all – a teaspoonful or so of peanut butter makes a great pick-up when spread on an oatcake mid-afternoon. But you get the energy boost minus quite a lot of calories if you stick to nuts.*

14

Energy black holes

One of the biggest energy drains in your life could be occupying the other half of your double bed.

Energy black holes are often the people around us — even the people we love. Dealing with their little ways can be exhausting. So what can you do?

First, make a list of the five people you spend most time with and ask yourself: 'How do I feel after spending an afternoon with them?' If the answer is 'exhausted', then you need to either avoid the person or shore up your energy reserves when you're with them and be very aware of the effect they have on you.

There are two types of 'black hole' – the *energy drainer*, who leaches away your energy, or the *energy enforcer*, who imposes their personality and needs all over your psyche so you end up exhausted. Here is an example of each type.

Here's an idea for you... Think of ways you can rephrase problems in your relationships so that you express what you *want* from the relationship. For instance say 'I want to have my ideas respected' rather than 'My boss is such a wet blanket'. Or 'I want to be equally responsible in our relationship' rather than 'My husband always decides where we eat'. It gives you a framework of how to behave in order to get what you want. The sentences that begin 'I' give you options; in the others, you're a victim of another's behaviours which, ultimately, you can't do anything to change.

THE 'YES, BUT ...' – AN ENERGY DRAINER

Everyone occasionally expresses doubts about a friend's suggestion. For the 'yes, but ...' crew, it's default mode. Whatever the decision, whatever the predicament, whatever suggestions are offered, the response of these people is always the same: 'Yes, but ...'. They always see problems. They never generate solutions. They always rain on your parade.

- *How to spot one.* Name just one time they were positive about any new plan, suggestion or person. No? You got one.
- *How they steal your energy.* You have to generate enough enthusiasm for both of you.

■ *How to deal with it.* Decide for yourself what action you'll take and present it to them. Before they can say 'yes, but …', whisk out the room and put your plan into action. In the long term it's worth seriously thinking whether you want them in your life at all. They are often lovely people, with our best interests at heart but, no matter how gentle their 'yes, but …', their basic fear of life holds back them, and everyone else they are associated with.

Take a look at IDEA 21, *How deep is your anger?* **– those energy black holes might be making you very angry.**

Try another idea…

THE CONTROL FREAK – AN ENERGY ENFORCER

People who only feel comfortable when they're making the ultimate decisions tend to be the ones in charge at home and at work. One of the supervisors I had was an energy enforcer. Being with her was absolutely exhausting – she talked so fast, wanted so much information, had so many ideas that I was like a boiled rag by the end of our sessions. When I realised what was going on, I took precautions – a double espresso before our session and an hour lying on the couch listening to classical music afterwards. She was worth it, because she taught me loads. At their best, control freaks keep the world turning round. The problems arise when they get so used to getting their own way that they forget that there is a valid alternative. Nobody else gets a look-in.

'Nobody realises that people expend tremendous energy merely to be normal.'
ALBERT CAMUS, philosopher

Defining idea…

- *How to spot one.* Think of a time when you did what you wanted to do with no argument or prevarication, or prior proof that their way wasn't working. In extreme cases, or where the freak is your boss, the answer might be 'never'.
- *How they steal your energy.* When they tip into bullies, and undermine your self-confidence.
- *How to deal with it.* Control freaks nearly always gravitate towards easy-going people. Most units can't handle two of them. Never give them a problem without suggesting a solution. Otherwise they'll stop focusing on the real problem and start thinking that you're the problem that they have to sort out. You really don't want to be taken over as a control freak's 'new project'. When they start trying to control something extremely important to you – how often you see your kids, or how often you have sex – you have to be very clear about what you think is reasonable, and that this is not just another encounter where you'll give in for an easy life.

Q   **What if my boyfriend is a 'yes, but ...'?**

A   *Of course, not all energy black holes should be excised from your life. But it's good to remember that it's always an option. With my supervisor, I only had to see her once a week. A boyfriend is more problematic. At the end of the day, each of us has to decide if the relationship with a black hole gives more than it takes away. You could explain to him the effect his behaviour has on you. Just don't waste energy trying to change him.*

Q   **I spend most of my time with my two children – two huge energy black holes. But that's kids for you, eh?**

A   *In what way do they drain your energy? You need to recognise when they are being energy drains and when energy enforcers. All children are energy drains sometimes. They get sick, they need to be played with, they wake in the night. Finding the energy to deal with that is part of being a parent. But when they flip into being energy enforcers – wilfully sapping your energy – that's different. My youngest child is a far stronger-willed character than me, but just because she's only six doesn't mean she has the right to enforce her energy at the expense of mine. I see children draining their parents' energy all the time – and the parents letting them. As soon as your children are old enough to understand the concept of 'fair play', they are old enough to understand that your energy deserves respect too.*

How did it go?

65

15

Avoid the brain drain

Are you feeling mentally sluggish? Having difficulty concentrating? Got an important exam or interview coming up, but feel like your brain has all the sharpness of a wet sponge? Then do this.

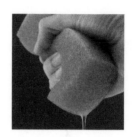

We can help. In just two weeks.

Brain ageing starts at a very young age, far younger than most of us imagine. How young? Your twenties, basically. No sooner has your brain stopped growing (late teens, early twenties) than it starts deteriorating. Ironic? No kidding. But given there's not much mileage in railing against evolution, what can we do about it?

'A lot' is the answer. Genetics is only about one-third of what predicts brain ageing, say the boffins at UCLA's Anti-Ageing Institute. The other two-thirds have to do with our environment and lifestyle choices.

RETRAIN YOUR BRAIN

If you're mentally sluggish and have trouble remembering not just where you left the car keys, but where you left the car, try this programme based on the latest research into brain drain. You can hope to see more mental sharpness within a few weeks.

Every morning

Chuck a handful of blueberries, prunes or raisins onto your cereal or porridge. These and other fruits and vegetables which have a deep-blue colour are particularly high in the 'ORAC scale'. The higher it is on the ORAC scale, the more brain-boosting anti-ageing antioxidants a food has.

Every day

Eat three meals and two snacks. Your brain needs a steady flow of fuel. Aim for at least one food supplying omega-3 oils – that's avocados, walnuts and, of course, fish. Or pop a supplement – either fish oil, or flax seed oil or evening primrose oil if you're a vegetarian. Limit saturated fatty foods – red meat and dairy.

Here's an idea for you... **Improve concentration: stick on some Mozart. Research from the University of California shows that people who listened to *Sonata for Two Pianos in D Major* while preparing for an IQ test scored higher than those who studied in silence. Mozart is the gold standard, but any rhythmic music will help as long as it doesn't have lyrics that disrupt concentration.**

Every couple of hours

De-stress. Cortisol is released when we're stressed and, according to Dr Small at UCLA, who has written several books on keeping your brain active, 'constant stress shrinks a key memory centre [in the brain]'. Every hour or so, stand up, take a deep breath and raise your arms above your head. Exhale and drop your arms. Repeat three times. This de-stresses your brain and your body as well as sending oxygen to your brain. Better still, when you are suddenly stressed and flooded with adrenaline, get into the habit of going for a brisk walk as soon as you can. As you know, sitting stewing in a foul mood makes it impossible to think straight – that's because cortisol actually inhibits your brain from working. Moving briskly 'burns off' the cortisol, allowing you to think straight again.

Turn to IDEA 22, H*erbal helpers* for details herbs that give physical and mental zing.

Try another idea…

Every two or three days

Go for a walk. Walking every two or three days for ten minutes, building up to forty-five minutes, was found to result in an improvement in mental agility. Stretching and toning exercises did not have this effect.

Health journalists have been twittering on for years about how doing puzzles like crosswords keeps the mind active into old age. It appears that we're wrong. Research does show that the brain can be retrained right into your eighties to learn new languages and skills – or indeed, how to do crosswords – but University of Virginia research shows that while mental challenges will keep you competent at doing those particular mental challenges, they will not necessarily stop Alzheimer's.

However, you can become sharper at mental challenges by practising. For instance, if you want to become better at sitting multiple-choice exams, guess what? Repeatedly practising multiple-choice questions will make you faster and better at them.

'If little else, the brain is an educational toy.'
TOM ROBBINS, American writer

Defining idea…

Set your brain a goal. Recall what the first three people you see were wearing. If you're told a phone number, work out a memory aid so you can dial it later. Invent another to help you remember the name of anyone you're introduced to (for example, if their name is Baker, imagine a loaf of bread on their head).

How did it go?

Q   I've been doing crossword puzzles for years in the belief that they'd keep me sharper. Are you saying that it's a waste of time?

A   *No. It will keep you good at crosswords. And almost certainly keep your brain sharper. It just won't guarantee that you're immune from dementia. You can pick up a language, learn to remember names and improve your memory so you don't forget your keys right into your eighties. That seems like a pretty good reason to continue.*

Q   What about gingko?

A   *The herb gingko biloba has been used for over 4000 years to give mental zing. A daily dose of 120–160mg may help improve concentration and memory as well as reducing mood swings and apathy. This is probably due to its positive effect on circulation and blood flow. It's worth trying as a supplement – but you will have to take it for at least a couple of months to notice an improvement. You can also get gingko supplements combined with ginseng which should help your physical and mental energy.*

16

Energise your bank balance

What do you think we worry about most? Relationships? Work? No, it's money.

Money has overtaken work as our biggest stressor. 51% of us are worried about money — it's a huge energy drain. Feeling you're on top of it will boost your energy overnight.

GOT SOME SPARE TIME? HERE ARE SOME IDEAS ON HOW TO FILL IT

In four hours: calculate how much you owe

Get all your bank and credit card statements together. Add up what you owe. Work out how long it will take to pay it off if you make minimum payments. If you're really brave, work out how much of that will be interest.

In four hours: deal with debts

Do you want to find the cheapest way to pay back your debts fastest? Transfer to a 0% credit card – although companies are beginning to make them less accessible. If

Here's an idea for you...

Buy a thermos food flask. Saving money on lunches is the sort of no-brainer move that, once you start, makes saving kind of fun. Look for other ways you can save yourself money without much effort. It helps you feel in control – and anything that does that is energising.

you don't want to pay transfer fees, you could try negotiating a lower rate with your present credit card company. Yes, they can do this – we just rarely ask. If you have a good payment history, they are more likely to take you seriously so it's easier if you pay by direct debit or always in time. When negotiating, if your first call centre bod doesn't seem too receptive, keep asking to talk to someone more senior. There is no guarantee that they will agree, but you may just get the enlightened person who realises that it's worth holding on to you as a customer.

In thirty minutes: open a savings account

The traditional wisdom is that it's daft to save if you still owe money. But I think it boosts your willpower and your mood to see money piling up. If you saved £100 a month in an online savings account or ISA paying 5%, that would be £6,829 in five

years – that's almost £1,000 in interest. Having a 'rainy day' fund is powerfully energising.

VERY IMPORTANT – For one month: write it down

The single best step you can make. Writing down everything you spend for a month will let you see where your money goes and give you a great sense that you're *doing something about your money.* Feeling you are taking control is in itself energising.

AND SOME MORE OBVIOUS STRATEGIES TO STOP MONEY DRAGGING YOU DOWN?

Bring home more

Your income should go up by inflation at least – but that doesn't mean you'll necessarily get a rise at work that equals inflation. A very rich self-help guru once gave me a tip and I've found it to be true. Decide how much you're going to earn at the beginning of each year, write it down, and you will find, magically, that the money appears. Even those of us on set incomes have the opportunity to earn more if we're prepared to think laterally. Spend most nights in a pub? Why not get a job in one? Or rent out a room in your home? You might enjoy it and, if you've a young family, a trustworthy person might do babysitting in return for a reduction in rent. Or clear out your garage and have a car-boot sale.

Give it up

And the alternative. I think you can count that your income has gone up 10% if you make savings of 10%, too. So when you really can't maximise your income any more – give up instead. Give up one holiday. Give up your car. Give up your tequila habit. There – better off already.

Being in control of your finances can take some doing. Read IDEA 20, *Willpower – it's all you need*, for more tips on how to get to where you want to be.

Try another idea…

'A bank is a place that will lend you money, if you can prove you don't need it.'
BOB HOPE, American comedian

Defining idea…

How did
it go?
Q **At the moment, I spend 50% of my income on holidays, going out, etc., but I don't have a mortgage. Is that OK?**

A *Terrific. Try to save a bit, but if you're quite happy spending your money on having a good time, why not? However, if you have a sneaky suspicion that you're throwing your money down the drain (majorly de-energising!), you could do something radical and pretend you have a mortgage already! By saving a chunk of your money as if for a mortgage, you'll soon have a whacking great deposit – which you can always blow travelling round the world, if you so wish. Just don't let the sense that your money is controlling you overwhelm you. That's the energy-draining bit.*

Q **But how do I budget?**

A *Here's a rough plan that works pretty well for most people as a basis. Some of these items will be fixed – for instance, housing. You may find you pay out more for mortgage, but at least you can see what percentage you will need to shave off another area. What's that? You have no idea what percentage you pay out for each item? That's what the spending diary and bank statements are for!*
- *35% on housing – mortgage or rent, plus insurance and upkeep*
- *15% on commuting – including car tax and insurance*
- *10% on savings*
- *15% on debt repayment*
- *25% on yourself*

17

The need for speed

And why it's draining your energy and eating up your life.

Make your new mantra 'slow, slower, slowest'. The slower you go, the faster you'll get there. If energy is your goal, that is.

The Slow Movement started in Italy twenty years ago. Now it's a worldwide movement that's got something to teach us all. Especially those of us who need more energy.

An Italian chef got fed up with the concept of 'fast food' and started the 'slow food' movement. Slow to cook, slow to eat. Better for you. Some other Italians had the idea of Cittaslow– a confederacy of cities dedicated to quality of life and making it a priority for people to meet each other, chat and relax. Then Carl Honore wrote *In Praise of Slowness* and the Movement got another lift.

Carl knows what it's like to live in the fast lane. So much so that when he saw a book of 'One-minute bedroom stories', his response was 'Yes!'. But that was his wake-up

Here's an idea for you... **Take off your watch tomorrow and see how you get on without it. You may well find that you still do all that you have to do in the right timeframe but the day goes slower. If you feel anxious at certain moments, ask yourself why. Treat it as a behavioural experiment to find out how much you are a slave to other people's agendas. Going watchless slows life right down but if it's too hardcore, then at least leave your watch off at weekends.**

call. 'Suddenly it hit me: my rushaholism has got so out of hand that I'm willing to speed up those precious moments with my son at the end of the day. That's why I began investigating slowing down.'

Why should you slow down? Because running full tilt at life can have a disastrous effect on your health. We need time to recoup. Not all the time. Just some of the time. And, actually, building periods of slowness into our day makes us more productive. That makes us feel better about ourselves meaning we've got more energy to enjoy life – note, I didn't say 'more energy to do more'. That's the one-minute-bedroom-story mentality.

Honore's idea is that speed has its place (we want a fast internet connection and train service) but in our 24/7 society it has got out of hand. What about you? Have you got the need for speed?

IN THE LAST WEEK, HAVE YOU ...

- Eaten a meal walking or standing up?
- Repeatedly pressed the button on the lift even when you know it doesn't make any difference?
- Walked up or down an escalator?
- Eaten *al desko* (at your desk)?
- Fallen asleep while commuting?
- Broken the speed limit?
- Packed most of your down time with activities you want to do/chores you have to do?

How many did you answer yes to?

IN THE LAST WEEK, HAVE YOU ...

- Lifted the phone to a friend who has been on your mind?
- Played with a child for longer than five minutes?
- Stayed in bed after the alarm has rung?
- Had a long bath?
- Just sat, doing nothing very much with a quiet mind?
- Deliberately switched off your mobile so you wouldn't be disturbed when you weren't doing anything else?
- Found the time to chat to a stranger?

How many did you answer yes to?

Read **IDEA 12**, *Give your brain a break*. **Relaxing your mind is a great way of slowing down.**

Try another idea...

'*Our obsession with speed is taking a terrible toll on our work, health, relationships and sex lives. The good news is that more people around the world are resisting the pressure to do everything in a hurry. And by slowing down they are living richer, fuller lives.*'

CARL HONORE

Defining idea...

Look at the ratio for the first section to the second section. If your ratio is pretty well equal or heavily in favour of the second section (unlikely unless you're a Buddhist monk), then your life may be hectic, but you know when to slow it down. Should it be heavily weighted in favour of the first section, try going slow.

SOME IDEAS

- Set your alarm fifteen minutes early and just lie in bed.
- Leave holes in your diary on every day of the week. Don't fill these holes up with stuff. Use them to relax.
- Take up a slow hobby – gardening, knitting, cooking, yoga. This is about the best thing you could do.
- When you're in a queue or at other dead times, try this. Close your eyes. Breathe in, breathe out. Do this nine times. There – instant meditation.

Q   I do like the idea but it's just not too practical for me. My 'to do' list is still half-done and I'm rushing around at full tilt. How can I possibly slow down?

How did it go?

A   *Start with baby steps. For instance you may not be able to give up eating ready-meals but you could cook one element of your evening meal from scratch – steam some carrots, peel an apple. You might not be able to take a bath rather than shower, but you could spend two extra minutes in the shower meditating on the water hitting the back of your neck. You might not be able to walk to work, but you could force yourself to stand still on the escalators and let your mind empty. Look for small ways to slow your life down and the rest will come, Grasshopper.*

Q   Oh God, shut up. Slow? Don't you know the very word makes me feel ill?

A   *Yes, I kind of know where you're coming from. During the research for this idea, even though I know it has value, I found my mind revolting against what I was reading. Try brainwashing yourself instead. Add a couple of slow websites to your internet 'favourites' and spend a minute browsing in the morning before you start work. Try www.slowlondon.com – not just for people who come from London. A little bit smug – mainly written by twenty-somethings who may be living fast lives, but rarely have to live fast lives. But having said that, it has some nice recommendations and, if nothing else, it will show you that there is an alternative.*

18

A one-minute answer to mid-afternoon slump

Practically every medical system in the world (with the exception of our own) believes that energy flows around the body in channels. Suspend disbelief!

Lack of energy is attributed to a block somewhere in this energy flow. Release the block and you get increased energy.

You can do this by applying needles, fingers or elbows to specific acupuncture points around the body.

True? Or unmitigated waffle? Here we're dealing with acupressure and there isn't scientific evidence that would pass muster with the *British Medical Journal* when it comes to acupressure and energy. However, there is evidence that acupressure works for helping with post-operative nausea and lower back pain – so working on the principle that if it works for one thing it may work for another, it's worth a try. I have derived benefit from the following facial massage which is specifically for tiredness and mental exhaustion. It was taught to me by a TCM (traditional

If mid-afternoon tiredness gets you down, combine the massage with this energising meditation – or do this instead of it. Empty your brain as far as possible, sit quietly, get an orange and concentrate on peeling it. Look at it first – orange is an energising colour. Smell it – citrus scents such as orange, bergamot and lemon are revitalising. Eat it – vitamin C and fructose make a wicked combination for energy. After your orange, drink a large glass of water. You should feel better in ten minutes.

Chinese medicine) doctor about twenty years ago. There may be a placebo effect going on here, but hey, who cares? Whatever gets you through the night or, in this case, through the afternoon. This is brilliant for mid-afternoon slump. I've since taught it to friends – specifically those who spend a lot of time at their desk– and many use it.

SHIATSU FACIAL MASSAGE FOR INSTANT ENERGY

- Lean your elbows on a table and let your face drop into your hands, with your palms cupped over your eyes. Look into the darkness formed by your hands. Stay there for as long as you feel comfortable or until your colleagues start to get worried.
- Place your thumbs on the inner end of each eyebrow and use your index fingers to work out along the upper edge of the eyebrow, applying pressure at regular intervals. When your index fingers reach the outer edge of your eyebrow, release all pressure.
- Return index finger to the inner end of each brow and work thumbs along to the *lower* end of the brows in similar fashion. Release as before.
- Place thumbs under ear lobes and apply pressure. At the same time, use the index fingers to apply pressure on points on a line from the bridge of the nose

under your eyes, along the ridge formed by your eye sockets.

- Touch fingertips to fingertips along an imaginary line running up the middle of your forehead from your nose to your hairline (no pressure is necessary). Use thumbs to apply pressure to points fanning out from the outer edge of the eyebrows to hairline. Repeat four times. (Feel for tender points and massage them. I find pressing on my temples when I'm stressed decreases tension in my jaw where, like a lot of people, I hold a lot of tension.)
- Use thumbs to apply *gentle* pressure in the eye sockets under the inner end of the eyebrow where you feel a notch at the ridge of the eye socket. (This is a very delicate spot. I was told by a doctor once that it is the major nerve closest to the surface of the body: I don't know if that's true, but go gently. You can really hurt yourself by pressing this point too hard.)
- Use one index finger to work up that imaginary line in your mid-forehead from the nose to your hairline.
- Now drop your head forward and, lifting your arms, work thumbs from your spine outwards along the ridge of your skull from the spine out to the point just under your earlobes. Do this four times.

OK, it's a bit of a faff to get the hang of the different points, but once you've practised a couple of times with the instructions, you'll have the hang of it. And it will be a good friend to your energy levels for the rest of your life.

For other one-minute wonders, look to IDEA 43, *Just a minute ...*

Try another idea...

'Shiatsu technique refers to the use of fingers ... to apply pressure to particular sections on the surface of the body for the purpose of correcting the imbalances of the body and maintaining and promoting health.'
Japanese Ministry of Health, Labor and Welfare, 1957.

Defining idea...

How did
it go?

Q   **It's a bit embarrassing – all this dropping your head in your hands. What if I don't want to do this at work?**

A   *Try this instead – not quite as effective in my experience, but worth a go. This reflexology point when massaged releases tension in the solar plexus, helps you breathe more deeply and reduces listlessness. Sit with a straight back, unsupported by the back of your chair. Use your thumb to work on your opposite hand. Find the fleshy part of your palm below the index finger and then go just below that. Press firmly for the count of four while breathing in, then release the point and your breath and breathe out for the count of four. Repeat at least four times.*

Q   **This is a lot of old balderdash, isn't it?**

A   *There are pictures of these sorts of techniques dating back to 3000 BCE. I find it quite touching that we're still using them today, although you may well be appalled at the thought. When you're tired and stressed and you don't have any other choice but to keep going, I think you could do a lot worse than try this out because at least it will give you a breather. A walk round the block might help, but sometimes we can't even leave our desks. Don't you think it's a bit short-sighted to dismiss shiatsu without at least having a shot at it?*

19
Unleash your sexual tiger – in just one week

You know sex would make you feel better if you could just muster up the energy to open your eyes.

Sex can be a good measure of your energy levels. The more you want, the better your energy levels as a general rule. But it works the other way too.

Sex raises your vitality, making you feel passionate and engaged with life. Boosting your libido so that you want more sex – and, yes, actually having more sex – can have a very positive effect on your energy levels.

Which is all very well, but according to one survey, one-third of us are too tired when we get into bed to do more than sleep.

This idea is based on the fact that, for many of us, it doesn't take too much to tip the hormonal balance in our favour. Working on the theory, and indeed the fact, that the more we think about sex, the more we want it, this is a one-week plan that forces you to think about sex just a little bit more. Prioritising it in your mind will

Here's an idea for you... **Swap the pillows to the end of the bed and have sex upside-down. Surprise releases the hormone dopamine, which increases friskiness, and swapping ends is the very easiest way to experience sex from a surprising new perspective.**

make you feel sexier and jolt you out of your 'take it or leave it' stance. You don't have to actually be with your partner for the magic to work. You've just got to consciously think about sex a little more.

Remember, you don't have to believe in it, for it to work ... just do it!

SEVEN DAYS TO TOTAL FULFILLMENT

Monday – Hop into the shower together

You may not have time to act on it, but getting lathered up together will get you thinking about sex, and that's a start.

Tuesday – Have breakfast in the garden

University of California research shows that libido is increased by 69% if you spend an hour a day outside. Start clocking up your minutes.

Wednesday – Buy apple strudel for dinner

Or any pudding that has cinnamon in it. The Smell and Taste Research Foundation in Chicago found that the smell is such an aphrodisiac that it increases the flow of blood to the bits that matter!

Thursday – Text your partner

Couples need to keep touching to release regular doses of oxytocin the bonding hormone. When you're away, 'virtual' strokes – with saucy or romantic texts – work nearly as well.

Turn to IDEA 26, *Lost that loving feeling?*, on what to do if the problem's more deep-rooted.

Try another idea...

Friday – Order garlic bread with lunch

Garlic contains allicin, which increases blood flow to the genitals and thus improves sensation and orgasms. Aim to eat a bulb crushed into food each week.

Saturday – Do the shopping

Go to www.sh-womenstore.com for some ideas. Go to www.lovehoney.co.uk or www.gash.co.uk for some inspiration. Even if you're not buying, browsing will get you thinking. And that's all you need.

Sunday – Turn up the central heating

Let your partner 'surprise' you walking around naked when they least expect it. It will give them a shock – let's hope a pleasant one –but the point is, it will get them thinking.

It is self-evident that by thinking about sex more you're going to be more likely to be in the mood that night. Someone who is thinking about chores, work and all they have to do the next day is naturally not going to be as up

'I'm too shy to express my sexual needs except on the phone to people I don't know.'
GARRY SHANDLING,
American Comedian

Defining idea...

87

for sex as someone who has allowed a few frisky thoughts to interrupt their routine. 'Making it different' is another simple way to keep it fresh between you. Try sleeping in front of the fire, in a tent in the garden, in the spare room. A little willingness to experiment can work wonders on your sexual energy levels.

How did it go?

Q   Isn't this is all a bit juvenile?

A   *Absolutely. The point of choosing a cinnamon pastry is that you're consciously thinking 'I'm doing something to boost my sex life' and that makes you feel more sexual. By all means ignore all of the above, as long as you substitute your own methods of thinking about sex more often and ways of surprising your partner. You could fantasise about someone you see on the bus. You could imagine you're someone else when you're with your partner tonight and act out how you think they would behave in bed (that should surprise them!). It doesn't really matter – just remember the mantra: 'think sex and surprise'. You're guaranteed to feel friskier.*

Q   Don't we just all lose interest in sex as we get older?

A   *Some of us do. About 60%, in fact. That's the percentage of people who may be genetically hardwired to get bored with sex as they age. So what do we do about it? Stopping having sex is an option, but not great if your partner is still interested. And, in my opinion, not a great option even then. Sex, like exercise, is often perceived as another drain on our energy when we're exhausted as it is. In fact, it is one of those activities that done with passion, enthusiasm and affection can actually energise us. Touch is pretty much a human essential for happiness, and we ignore it at our peril.*

20

Willpower – it's all you need

In order to make the lifestyle changes that will ensure you have boundless energy, you need one magic ingredient – willpower.

You know, you know. You're fed up with my nagging. If you're not eating breakfast, getting to bed early, giving up your addiction to Sky Sports and (most especially) exercising regularly, you are living but half a life.

IF ONLY IT WASN'T SUCH A FAG

So this idea is about giving you a mental image to strengthen your motivation. Once I interviewed a self-help guru who used a phrase that tickled me. I can't remember much of the rest of what he said, but he described the need 'to use your willpower like a karate chop'. Short, sharp, just do it.

I think it's a good metaphor. Times when I can't be bothered, I see myself decked out in a karate outfit, chopping planks of wood with my bare hands. That's the

Here's an idea for you... **Build up your willpower in small bites. Promise yourself that you will achieve one task tomorrow. Keep it really simple, something you can't fail at: eating an apple, flossing your teeth, reading your child a bedtime story. Every night make yourself a promise and keep it. If you fail, pick something easier the next night. Willpower is like a muscle: the more you use it, the larger it grows. Soon you'll be keeping big promises too.**

sort of decisiveness you need to muster if you're going to change long-engrained habits that aren't helping your energy levels. And if the thought of having willpower like a karate chop is making you shake your head in disbelief, try this. It turns you into a Man (or Woman) of Steel.

Step 1   Notice distractions

Some of us make up our minds to do something, and it's as good as done – about 1% of the population: quite possibly the self-made millionaires and serial killers. The rest of us, meanwhile, have minds like kites in the wind, blown around by whatever catches our attention. I am not a lazy person, but I am very, very, very easily distracted. If you're like me, you will be helped by becoming aware of it. Notice when you sit down to work how you are distracted by the urgent need to know what's on TV this evening. Notice when you are pulled away from that healthy salad by the siren song of the focaccia and double cheese. Notice when you were just about to go out for a walk, but your best friend called, and by the time you'd finished chatting, it was dark. Don't do anything just yet ... only notice.

Step 2   Learn the mantra

This is your own personal reminder to yourself to complete what you've started. It is a
sentence you say out loud as often as you need
to but most especially when you notice you
are being distracted. You will have to find one
that works for you but you're welcome to borrow mine which is: 'My intention now
is to …' Fill in the blanks. Saying it out loud is crucial. It's like you've made a promise
and it seems to stick.

Step 3   Get out of your comfort zone

This is the hard bit. Now we're going to prove to yourself that you're not a wuss
incapable of making the changes you need to make in order to get your energy
back. Next time you're in the shower, turn the temperature control from hot to
cold for one second. NB. You have to be under the water at the time or it doesn't
count. Each day turn the water on cold for just a bit longer. Work up gradually until
you can stay under the shower for one whole minute. Once you've managed to
stand under the cold water for 60 seconds, try an experiment next morning: turn
the shower back to cold for just ten seconds. It will seem like a complete breeze.
Your comfort zone has extended. You have exerted your self-control like a dynamic
karate chop. And the memory will stay with
you, building your self-esteem and pushing
you on to achieve other good stuff. Soon you
will be bounding off that comfort zone which
is your couch and running gazelle-like round
the park instead.

Try another idea…

Apply this along with **IDEA 8,**
*How to start exercising when
you really don't want to*, and
you'll be a *bona fide* exerciser
in no time.

Defining idea…

'**It is not that some people
have willpower and some
don't. It's that some people
are ready to change and
others are not.**'
JAMES GORDON, American physician

How did it go?

Q **How on earth is having a cold shower going to make me exercise regularly?**

A *This sounds like a physical idea but it's actually a mental one. If you have tried over and over again to make changes in your life and failed, that's a big backlog of disappointment in yourself. And, let's face it, it's simply a failure to achieve what you want to achieve. This cold-shower business isn't easy for any but the most masochistic of us, but it does change round your idea of yourself.*

It's well worth cultivating because, once you can gather your willpower and then unleash it with explosive power on whatever task you want to achieve, you'll find it immensely useful in everything from resisting that last pint in the pub to saving for a pension rather than blowing your excess loot on frivolous handbags, boy toys and the like.

Q **Getting out of the comfort zone sounds good. Is it?**

A *It's doubly energising. As well as giving you greater belief in your ability to get things done, getting out of your comfort zone in one area makes you more interested in doing it in others. You'll become more open to new experiences, more interested in life, more open to change and less boring.*

21

How deep is your anger?

We can expend an awful lot of energy being angry. It affects our energy levels in two important ways.

First, being angry uses up a lot of energy. Secondly, suppressing anger is a huge energy drain. So whether you're always getting angry, or you don't get angry enough, understanding how anger affects your energy levels is worthwhile.

Once I worked with a woman who got ridiculously worked up by her landlord. She would come into work once a week incandescent, practically spitting with rage, with some story of his irrational and unreasonable behaviour. I still don't know who she was really angry with, but I'm pretty sure it wasn't just with the insignificant sins of the landlord.

Here's an idea for you...

Frustrated? Angry? But don't want to expend mental energy on it? Try this. It's a form of 'mindful meditation' used by professional sportsmen who don't want to lose focus when things go wrong. Begin to describe every movement you are making as if explaining it to a blind person. 'I'm walking along the pavement, I'm taking deep breaths. I'm very upset that bus went by without stopping for me but I'm noticing that the sky is a nice shade of blue.' It pulls you out of pointless anger, fast.

If you are constantly fighting with one person, or unprovoked anger is released by one kind of situation or type of person (say a traffic warden or policeman), stop and ask yourself 'What's this about?'. The therapy question would be: 'What does this person mean to me?'

Who or what does the situation or person signify to you, or remind you of? It can help to write down what's making you angry, and when you get to the stage of writing 'This reminds me of …' or 'This is just like the time when …', pay attention. You could be near finding out why certain situations trigger your anger. Common ones are when you get angry in situations where: you feel you are being disrespected; you're being expected to find all the solutions; you feel bullied or manipulated; you aren't being allowed to take control.

When the trigger is recognised for what it is, its power often melts away.

'THE ONE WHO ANGERS YOU, CONTROLS YOU'

This is the saying of a woman I know, who uses it as the reason never, ever to lose her temper. If she shows her anger, she feels the person she's angry with has control of her, has won. I'm not sure of this as a strategy. It works as long as you are aware of your anger and express your inner feelings, albeit in a calm way. It doesn't work if you don't acknowledge your anger and pretend it doesn't exist. All of us feel anger, but some of us feel very unsafe admitting it. There are psychological reasons for this and yes, you guessed it, they often go back to your childhood. If you weren't 'validated' – paid attention to, listened to, acknowledged – you grow up believing that your feelings don't matter much and that there's no point in expressing them. When it comes to 'bad' feelings you actually think that if others suspect they exist, you'll be rejected even further. This is something it's worth knowing about yourself, because keeping a lid on all this rage takes a huge amount of energy.

Answer each of these questions. For every 'Often', score 3; 'Sometimes', score 2; and 'Rarely, if ever', score 1.

1   I'm often angry but no one would know.
2   When I'm angry, I cry.
3   I find myself telling myself not to get angry.
4   I have been so angry that I can't get to sleep.
5   I don't see the point of getting angry in public.
6   If I do express anger, I'm very disap-
     pointed in myself afterwards.

If you scored 15–18: You may feel low-level anger a lot of the time and life feels a bit helpless or

Idea 14, *Energy black holes*, has more on energy draining emotions.

Try another idea...

'Anger is always a response to perceived injustice, which may dissolve with deeper understanding.'
MARTHA BECK, life coach and author

Defining idea...

hopeless. Learned helplessness is part of your repertoire for dealing with problems. This may take a great deal of energy.

If you scored 10-14: You know when you're angry but you rarely find the space to let it out. It could affect your energy levels if you're under pressure, too.

If you scored 9 or under: You're anger is usually acknowledged, acted on and released. It probably doesn't impact too much on your energy.

SAFE WAYS TO DEAL WITH ANGER

- Talk to a friend. Really let go. Tell your friend that you don't want solutions – at least at first. You just want them to listen. If you don't have anyone who can do this for you, you need a counsellor.
- Write it down. Scribble three pages of A4 without stopping. Don't edit. Just pour it out.
- Scream. Really loudly. The car's a good place.

Q I'm often left feeling tearful by my sister. She is mean and vindictive towards me. I seem to be paralysed during her attacks. Then she waltzes off. That's when I get angry, but it's too late, and my mood slumps after the anger has passed. What can I do?

How did it go?

A *Rerun in your mind different times this has happened. Look for points in the interaction where you could step in and turn around the situation by behaving differently. Play-act in front of a mirror different ways you could behave that would ensure you don't find yourself in that situation again. Practise what you could say, how you could react, to get a different outcome. Studies have shown that there isn't necessarily anything that terrible about suppressing anger, as long as we acknowledge that's how we feel and make it known – in other words, turning anger into assertiveness.*

Q **Getting angry boosts my energy. I like it. Can I keep it?**

A *This isn't necessarily a bad thing. My partner gets angry when he's tired but still has physical work to do. He subconsciously gets himself wound up, stressed out and then gets on with what he's got to do as a way of burning off the adrenaline induced by the stress reaction. It's not a terrible strategy since he doesn't use it that often. Otherwise it might well raise his blood pressure. However, if he is tired and has has mental or emotional work to do, it's rubbish for giving him the energy he requires. He gets wound up but can't concentrate or sit still. So, use anger to raise your energy levels with care. Sometimes it works. Sometimes it doesn't.*

22

Herbal helpers

Tonics have been used for millennia to pep us up when we're defunct of energy. But how much good are they, really?

There is some evidence that tonics do have a valuable place, especially if you are facing a period of particular stress and hard work.

GINSENG

The 'big daddy' of energy boosting supplements, it supports your body when you're going through emotional and physical stress. Energy levels improve as well as over-all stamina, concentration and resilience.

Some studies have shown that fatigue, anxiety and poor concentration are all helped by ginseng; but it has to be said that some have shown no positive benefits. It did help nurses in one study cope with the energy drain associated with swapping from day shifts to night shifts, but the study was small. Personally, ginseng helps me cope with stress – I'll start taking it when I know I have a particularly difficult time ahead. It could well be a placebo – but so what? It helps me stay calm and focused when times get tough.

Korean ginseng

Panax ginseng or Korean ginseng is used as general tonic to restore fatigue, anxiety, nervousness and poor concentration. I've used it myself with no side effects whatsoever, but in some women it can cause menstrual-related symptoms (including breast tenderness). For this reason, Panax ginseng isn't suitable for some (look to Siberian ginseng, mentioned below).

Buy the most expensive ginseng you can find or afford. If it seems really cheap, the chances are there's a reason, most probably that it doesn't contain any ginseng at all. Read the label and look for 4–7% *ginsengosides* if possible. The optimum dose is 200mg twice daily, taken in split doses of 100mg each. Traditionally, it's recommended that you don't take it routinely but on occasional, two- to three-weekly courses, maximum one month, whenever you feel that your energy is flagging or you need to optimise it. Then have a gap of a few weeks. There are now some supplements designed to be taken all year round.

Here's an idea for you… **Try ginseng tea. It's a refreshing pick-up that works out cheaper than supplements. You can buy teabags or you can prepare an infusion. Add 1 dessertspoonful of dried ginseng root to a cup of boiling water. Leave for five minutes. Drink up to four cups a day.**

Side effects include headaches, irritability and nervousness, insomnia and the menstrual symptoms mentioned above. Korean ginseng shouldn't be taken by those with heart conditions or taking oestrogen or corticosteroids because it may increase their action. Those with diabetes and other conditions requiring medication should always speak to their pharmacist first.

Siberian ginseng

Its proper name is *Eleutherococcus*; it is milder than Panax ginseng and is suitable for every-one. Siberian ginseng is actually a completely different plant from Panax so it might work for you if Panax doesn't. Its main uses are as a tonic for fatigue and it also has been researched extensively as an immune booster, so if you keep getting one cold after another, it's worth trying. You won't be surprised to find out that most of the research into Siberian ginseng took place in the Soviet Union, not the West, and the results were pretty uniformly fabulous, which is always suspect when it comes to trials so they can't be totally believed.

However, in one study it did appear to reduce incidence of flu by more than 90% over the seven years of the trial so if repeated infections are draining your energy, give it a go. The standard dose is 2–4 ml of the tincture up to three times a day. Take for two months then take a two- to three-week break.

Side effects are pretty rare but include insomnia, melancholy and anxiety.

Vitamin supplements can give a boost to energy too. Turn to IDEA 39, *Big in Japan*.

Try another idea…

Rhodiola

Rhodiola is not well known. Like ginseng it is a herbal remedy for tiredness, and there are studies that back up its reputation as an energy booster. It contains a group of distinctive compounds called rosavins that appear to enhance the activity of a number of brain chemicals. (Look for the word 'standardised' to describe the rosavin on the label.)

'Energy is the eternal delight.'
WILLIAM BLAKE, poet and mystic

Defining idea…

The most significant study (but still a very small one) is of 40 Russian medical students given rhodiola before exams. They reported that they had more energy as well as feeling happier than a group taking a placebo. Rhodiola has had a folk-culture reputation in Asia and parts of Europe for generations (its other name there is Arctic root).

How did it go?

Q   What about ginseng's aphrodisiac qualities?

A   *Ginseng causes release of nitric oxide (as do onions and Viagra). If you're a man suffering from tiredness in the bedroom, try 300mg of Korean red ginseng for three months. In a small study of 30 men, an increase in sexual performance after this dose was reported.*

Q   Anything else worth trying?

A   *The Indian Ayurvedic medicine tonic, ashwagandha, is often compared with ginseng, and sometimes more favourably. It fights fatigue and reduces inflammation as well as restoring calm. In one double-blind study 101 men in their fifties took ashwagandha for a year. Mineral levels were restored to those of younger men, they reported that the rate at which their hair was greying slowed down, and 70% of the men in the tonic group had increased libido. In animal studies, this tonic has been found to increase energy when under physical and mental stress.*

23

Think before you drink

Let's not get too hysterical about alcohol. But let's think about it.

No one's saying give it up. But if your energy levels aren't high, it's one of the obvious energy drainers.

Alcohol (any old alcohol, not just wine) does your heart good. Probably not quite as much as is claimed. For instance, women can only expect the benefits of alcohol to kick in after the menopause, and even then, more than one or two drinks a day is probably detrimental, rather than beneficial.

Having said that, there is even some evidence that it could do your energy levels good. A Spanish study of nearly 20,000 adults found that drinking moderately meant increased sense of wellbeing and less sickness than teetotallers.

But once you get over that moderate one or two into three or four, the bad side kicks in. Less oxygen reaches your cells because alcohol causes dilation of the blood vessels. You could become dehydrated – alcohol is a powerful dehydrator. And your liver has to work hard to metabolise it if you drink to excess.

Then of course, there's the danger of hangover.

Here's an idea for you... **What's your drinking rate? Your liver can process one unit of alcohol an hour. Stick to that and fill up with water for the rest of the time. You'll find you feel more in control, you may never have a hangover again and you'll have more energy the next day.**

The pounding headache of a hangover is down to dehydration. Even a very slight thirst means you have already lost 1% of your body's fluid and two cups of water are needed to replace it. When you reach hangover levels of dehydration your body is screaming for pints of fluid. Alternate a glass of still water with every alcoholic drink.

Milk thistle is a natural detoxifier that helps the liver to function optimally. Take the herb before and after drinking alcohol.

HANDLING ALCOHOL ON A DAILY BASIS

Let's face it, being a teetotaller is very hard in our society. For some of us, it's harder than others. I know one journalist who, when he's with his work colleagues, actually pretends to be a reformed alcoholic so no one forces him to drink. 'I just couldn't hack the amount that some of my colleagues drink and remain functioning. I don't know how they do it.' This isn't a bad strategy. He's happy to drink at home with his wife – just not with what he calls the 'booze monsters'. Here are some strategies that might help.

- Alcohol cuts down on oxygen and this leads to tiredness – both mental and physical. Don't slouch over your pint. Breathe deeply. This is a lot safer now that more pubs are banning smoking.
- Carry *Nux vomica* – a homeopathic remedy that stops nausea and headaches.

- Fruit juice is your best friend: it is full of the antioxidants that help strengthen the liver; fructose increases the speed at which the body metabolises alcohol; and vitamin C is a natural energiser.

Need more willpower? See IDEA 20, *Willpower – it's all you need*.

Try another idea...

- Watch out for high-sugar drinks like sherry and alcopops. The sugar means they're absorbed into the blood stream faster and eliminated more slowly, so you get more drunk faster – and stay that way longer. Brandy, oaked Chardonnays and young red wines may also be high in compounds called congeners that are hard on the body, and take more energy to metabolise.

- Eat before you go out – it will cut down the effects of alcohol and save you calories too. If you're full, you're less likely to get drunk, or to become a victim of 'the munchies' and start scoffing nibbles to keep going. I've followed the advice of nutritionist Amanda Ursell, who told me to eat beans on toast as a stomach liner, and it works excellently well – not filling you up too much, but minimising alcohol's bad effects.

AND IF IT ALL GOES WRONG?

Give your liver a makeover. This will help you recover your energy the day after, faster.

Take 600–1000mg of milk thistle throughout the day. This strengthens the outer membranes of liver cells. Research at the Cedars-Sinai Medical Centre in LA shows that, if you take milk thistle in the days before a big drinking session, it reduces hangovers.

Take 1200mg of N-acetyl-cysteine. This dose was reported by the *New Scientist* to completely banish hangover symptoms.

'One martini is all right. Two are too many. Three are not enough.'

JAMES THURBER,
American humourist

Defining idea...

Take 75mg of vitamin B complex, 500–1000mg of vitamin C and 2 g of evening prim-rose oil before you go out, and repeat the morning after. This may help reduce the effects of hangover by replacing destroyed vitamins.

How did it go?

Q   I've tried to give up alcohol before but to no avail. What now?

A   *The herb kudzu could help. It reduces alcohol cravings. A trial in the UK discovered it helped 64% of people to cut down. But we're not talking about giving up here; we're talking about cutting down. And if you can't cut down, you may have something to worry about. Has anyone you care about ever expressed worry about the amount you drink? This is often the first sign that our drinking is getting out of control.*

Q   Are there some alcoholic drinks that are more energising than others?

A   *Technically no. Alcohol is alcohol is alcohol – and all of it is a depressive. But some drinks do seem to affect your mood in different ways. Champagne is well-known for lifting the spirits – it must be the bubbles. I remember feeling very 'energetic' after a few caipirinhas (that's a Brazilian cocktail made with rum, sugar cane and pure lime juice). Now when you think of it that makes sense: sugar would hit your blood stream and give you an immediate 'hit', and vitamin C is another instant energiser. So if you're feeling a bit flat before a party, try these. Just be prepared for the crash that follows.*

24

Good morning, sunshine

Here's the simplest yoga routine, that's been energising people for thousands of years.

Time spent mastering this move could be one of the best investments you make in terms of energy.

One reason its fans love yoga so much is that it gives them energy. This specific effect on energy levels has been backed up by research. The *Journal of the Royal Society of Medicine* reported on the effects on participants' mood and vitality in three groups of volunteers: some did relaxation exercises, some visualisation and some yoga. Those doing a 30-minute programme of yoga reported an increase in both mental and physical energy. They also reported a lift in their mood. They were more alert; the other groups reported feeling more sluggish and less happy.

You don't have to do much yoga to benefit. The 'Salute to the Sun' is just that – it's meant to be carried out while facing the rising sun. But wherever you do it, it's specifically designed to increase your energy. That said, this is a brilliant way of starting your day: it releases tension, limbers up the body after sleep and stimulates circulation before your day.

Here's an idea for you...

Yogic breathing has been shown in some studies to 'wake up' your brain, specifically those parts responsible for creativity and logical thinking. Close off your right nostril with the thumb of your right hand and breathe in through your left for the count of four. Now close off your left nostril with the index finger of your right hand and exhale for the count of four. Breathe in through your right nostril, and then out through your left, closing off your right nostril with your thumb. Repeat half a dozen times. This is great for relaxing you at any time of the day.

If possible, do this outside, facing the sun, first thing. Failing that, your bedroom's fine. Stand straight and tall, feet bare and about a foot apart. Hold your hands, pointing upwards, in front of your chest as if you were praying.

1   *Inhale* and lift your arms straight above your head, stretching backwards a few centimetres so that you feel a stretch across your front.

2   *Exhale*. At the same time, bend forwards from your hips so that your hands are on each side of your feet. You may have to bend your legs slightly at the knee until you get more flexible.

3   *Inhale*. At the same time, place your right foot behind you as far as you can. Then place your left foot there too, so that your hands and feet are supporting your body.

4   *Exhale*. At the same time, lower your knees to the floor, then your chest, then your chin. You should look as if you are about to do a press up.

5   *Inhale*. At the same time, slowly straighten your arms and arch your back from the waist so your chest is lifted off the floor.

6   *Exhale*. At the same time, push back onto your knees, tuck your toes in, then straighten your arms and legs so that you make an inverted V, standing on your toes.

7   *Inhale* and step between your hands with your left foot.

8   *Exhale* and step between your hands with your right foot.

9   *Inhale*. At the same time, slowly return to the standing position.

Couple this with a good breakfast for a great start to your day. See IDEA 35, *Eat breakfast*.

Try another idea...

Now repeat. Take your time to learn how to do this properly. The breathing is important. But with practice you should be able to do this between 10 and 20 times in a minute. The more you do it, the more energy you gain. Once you've got the hang of it, swap the leg you lead with from stage 3 (right first, then left) – but I found it helped to get the hang of it one way before I started mixing it up.

One result of all the upward and downward movements, say yoga adherents, is that they strengthen the adrenals, those glands that we depend on for energy and which are overworked by stress. The 'Salute to the Sun' is a marvellous, instant tonic but taking up a regular class and beginning your own practice, as it's called, will benefit you more.

Does yoga deliver? I've met some yoga practitioners who weren't as relaxed, enlightened and serene as they thought they were. But I've never met one who didn't look fabulous. So that's a nice secondary benefit.

'I got into yoga late, when I was 38 or 39. I wish I'd started earlier.'

STING

Defining idea...

Q   Is doing this really enough to get benefits?

A   *Try it and see. A couple of weeks of 'Salute to the Sun' can revolutionise your morning. This is a starter. American research shows that just twenty-five minutes of yoga dramatically decreases tension levels and blood pressure. Classes with a qualified teacher are much better and there is a wealth of information on different types of yoga easily available these days. Do some research until you find the type that most appeals to you, or ask friends for recommendations.*

Q   I'm not terrific in the morning. Can't I do it later?

A   *You shouldn't do this in the evening – it's too energising! But other yoga moves make a great tension-reliever before bed. I once did a yoga class at 10pm and I've rarely slept so well. However, what you want is energy, not stress reduction. If bad sleep is draining your energy, find some yoga moves suitable for the evening. If not, then persevere with the morning – it's only five minutes and breaking out of your comfort zone may help energise you in other ways.*

25

Dealing with interruptions

Other people and their agendas – they suck the energy right out of you. But there are ways of dealing with interruptions.

It's been one of those days. This morning I had a clear day to get on with writing this. And then it all went wrong.

I've taken two phone calls and been side-tracked at the school gates by a friend wanting a coffee and a chat. I've agreed to pick up another parent's kid, which shouldn't be a problem but, somehow, now it is. It's now 12.45 pm and I've written 100 words. (That's not good, by the way.)

I'm reminded of the definition of an optimist: someone who believes that today will be better than yesterday. What's the definition of a fantasist? Someone who believes today will be better even if she doesn't make any changes. Sure, I can be an optimist, imagining I'll zip through everything I want to achieve today, but if yesterday was constantly hijacked by other people, and I don't do anything to change that today, I'm living on Fantasy Island if I think I'll get everything done.

And that feeling of having wasted time is a total energy bummer. So it's time to start making some plans to ensure that I don't let other people interrupt me. My trigger points will be different from yours – as you've probably guessed, mine is

Here's an idea for you...

Over the next week, note down when you were interrupted, by whom and for how long. At the end of the week, go through marking those interruptions that you couldn't put off because they were too important. How long did you have to spend dealing with them? Next week be aware when you're planning your week's workload that that amount of time may 'disappear' from any day because of critical interruptions. Keep a note to see if it's the same next week. Planning for interruptions that can't be avoided means your week will flow more easily.

being seduced by my friends into going off-track. Below we explore some possible energy drains, and what hopeless cases – and that means me – can do about it.

YOU WORK IN AN OFFICE

The average office worker is interrupted every three minutes, according to research under-taken in California. It's a wonder that we get anything done at all. If you're lucky enough to have your own office space, how about operat-ing a one-hour-door-open, one-hour-door-shut policy, when you can't be interrupted. It's also worth learning some great exit lines for bouncing the interrupter back to the drawing board until it suits you and/or they find some-one else to help them. You could try 'Sorry, got to finish this project; can we talk about it tomorrow?' or 'Sorry, this week is impossible; what about next week.'

YOUR HOBBY IS CHATTING

Yep, this is me. The answer is simple. Just say no. Personally, knowing how weak I am, I don't engage in conversation. Tomorrow, unlike today, I won't answer the phone but let the machine pick up. I'll check messages for urgency at noon and five o'clock.

YOU'RE A 'SOCIAL E-MAILER'

This tag is the invention of my friend Jane Alexander, a wonderful writer who admits that one of her occupations is 'social e-mailer'. She lives in the depths of Devon, so for her there's some excuse: e-mail is her window on the world. For the rest of us, it's probably nothing but a huge distraction. One radical idea that works for me is not to look at e-mails first thing in the morning. Instead, spend that first hour doing the most important task of the day. Often that first hour is the calmest you'll get, and what do you spend it doing? 'Chatting' to your friends – it's just that the written word fools you into thinking you're working. Or else you're answering other people's banal requests. Try ignoring your e-mails until you've done some serious work, and check them no more than three times a day.

YOU CAN'T SAY 'NO'

Perhaps you need to look at whether you are just being helpful or are hooked on being needed. Next time, when you're tempted to let yourself be distracted, ask yourself 'if I respond to this distraction, who am I disappointing?' It might be your boss, it might be you, it might be the child that you won't be able to take to the park at the weekend because you'll be making up time on a work project instead. Seeing the human cost of allowing yourself to be interrupted can help you decide if it's worth it or not.

Addicted to changing your plans? Read IDEA 30, What *kind of a time traveller are you?* You may be a P.

Try another idea…

'I choose to … live so that which came … to me as a blossom, goes on as a fruit.'
DAWNA MARKOVA, poet

Defining idea…

How did it go?

Q **I've been taking your advice and saying to interrupters, 'Look, I've only got 5 minutes', but it's not working. Why?**

A *Limiting interruptions is **not** my advice – it's a must. According to one piece of research, it can take up to 25 minutes to regain our concentration fully after an interruption, and another study found that if we're interrupted in the middle of a train of thought, 40% of the time we don't return to the original project. We need a zero-tolerance policy. Don't enter into it at all.*

Q **But sometimes you can't help being interrupted, can you?**

A *One way of getting over the inertia of returning to the project is to adopt a trick used by professional writers to guard against writers' block. Stop in the middle of a sentence so that, as soon as you sit down, you know where to start. It makes it a lot easier than a sheet of white paper. You can adapt this to whatever work you do.*

26

Lost that loving feeling?

When you've misplaced your mojo, it's a drain on your physical and emotional resources.

Reconnecting is important because when you're not having sex, and you don't know why, you're missing out on one of life's great energisers.

It's a lot easier than you might think to drift into a disaster situation in your relationship, where you're with each other but not *with* each other. Luckily, it can be just as simple to reconnect.

STEP 1

Are you out of sync? Might you as well be living in different time zones for all the meaningful contact you have with one another? Do you have commitments that mean you can't be together at the same time, whether that's in the morning or evening? Children pull away a lot of the energy that you used to have for each other.

Here's an idea for you... **Are you feeling low? In women who were mildly depressed, taking the herb St John's Wort improved their mood – and in 60% of cases, it also had the effect of boosting their libido.**

Are you booking a regular babysitter at least once every two weeks and spending time together, just the two of you?

Fix it tonight

Go to bed at the same time. Some people can live in different countries and keep their love alive, but you may not be two of them. Lots of couples lose it because one partner goes to bed and one stays up playing with the remote control. Get into bed at the same time and talk to each other. See what happens.

STEP 2

Get real. This isn't terrific or easy to do, but take a long look in the mirror – metaphorically and literally. Cast your mind back to when you met your partner. Who were you? What were you doing? That's the person your partner fell in love with, and maybe you need to bring more of that energy back into your present persona. Now, literally, look at yourself. In a big mirror, naked. If you're not quite in the buff condition you were when you met your partner, it doesn't mean they've gone off you. But it could mean you've gone off yourself.

Illness affects your libido. Look at IDEA 48, *Tired ... or ill?*, for some clues as to what might be draining your energy and sex drive.

Try another idea...

Looking your absolute best, taking time and care with your appearance, wearing clothes (and underwear and nightclothes) that make you feel sensual and erotic can't fail to make you feel more sexual. Your partner may not notice (then again, he or she might be pathetically grateful), but you certainly will. Don't underestimate the power of the shallow and superficial.

Fix it tonight

Go through your wardrobe and chuck anything that doesn't make you look good or feel good. If it's old, tired, too comfy or unattractive, chuck it out. You may be left with three items of clothing – but you'll look and feel hot in them.

STEP 3

In the words of Prince, think sexy. Think about sex more often. It's generally accepted that men want sex more than women (though I wouldn't always bet on it) and surprise, surprise, they think about it more. If you're a woman who spends more time thinking about what you're going to make for dinner than how inspiring your sex life is, it's not surprising you're not feeling

'Women need a reason to have sex. Men just need a place.'

BILLY CRYSTAL, comedian

Defining idea...

117

like sex much. This isn't a criticism. Life is busy, but our love life should be a pretty high priority.

Fix it tonight

Remember the last time you had sex. Remember the best time. Remember how it felt the first time you really wanted someone. Remember anything as long as it's a strongly sexual memory. Stay with the memory for five minutes. And revisit it every hour, on the hour. That's who you are. Find the passionate you again.

STEP 4

Now it's time to talk and ask. Ask for more love. Ask for you partner to make it a priority for them too. If he or she is too stressed or too tired, then you need to help and support each other to find time to be together and reconnect. Perhaps you need to cut something else out of your life. Maybe switching off the television is all it takes.

Fix it tonight

Couples absolutely need time alone. Decide on a date and make it happen. If you can't get a regular babysitter, ask a friend to watch the kids for a couple of hours on a Saturday afternoon or even as soon as you get home from work. Then high-tail it back to bed. If it's been a long time since you made love and you're shy, just hold each other and talk about what's going on for you and why it's got so difficult.

Q **None of this worked. My husband is still very withdrawn. Any ideas?**

How did it go?

A *Is something else going on? Is he ill? On drugs? Depressed? Has he got secrets? None of us really know what's going on inside another person, even those we spend the most time with. Forget about sex, and just start with getting him to communicate. Switch off the TV, put the kids to bed and each write down one thing that you love about your partner, and one thing you want to fix in your relationship. Really listen – don't dismiss or argue with the good stuff, and don't get defensive about the bad. Talk about what comes up.*

If he won't do this, you need to look at your options. Can you stay in this sort of marriage? Lots do. If not, suggest counselling for him or for you as a couple. And be very clear what the consequences will be if nothing changes.

Q **My wife doesn't think sex is necessary when you reach our age. I'm trying every way I can gently to tell her that without sex we don't have a marriage. Am I right?**

A *You sound kind of demanding and that is a real turn off for a lot of us. I don't blame you for wanting sex, but blackmailing your wife isn't the way to go. She may have all sorts of reasons for the 'our age' viewpoint. Have you asked her if sex has become painful or unpalatable to her? All of this requires real gentleness: allow her to really explore what's going on for her with no pressure. You do have a right to physical affection, if not sex, and you might be surprised how much closer you two grow if you cuddle her without demanding sex. Physical contact is sometimes necessary to get the libido working again, but it's a long process. Don't rush it.*

119

27

Never run out of energy again

Welcome to the energy scale. This simple idea is based on a technique used in cognitive behavioural therapy.

Adapting it to focus on your energy levels means you never need to get too exhausted again.

Chronically depressed people are taught by therapists to keep a weather eye on their depression, to check in on the levels as it fluctuates throughout the day (because mood fluctuates, and even the severely depressed have times when they are less depressed). This means that when they begin to observe signs that they are getting more depressed; they can take steps to pull themselves back up and thus avoid spiralling down into a trough.

I don't suffer from depression, but I do get tired and overwhelmed, and I have found that adapting this technique to work for my energy levels is invaluable in keeping them balanced and avoiding a slump.

Stock up on yoghurt! Studies in the US show that eating it daily improves alertness levels.

First, shut your eyes for a few minutes and imagine your energy. What does it look like? You're looking for a metaphor that you can zone into whenever you need to, so it has to be true for you. It might be a deep well that's brimming with water when you're full of bounce, but empty and dry when you're depleted. It could be a gigantic ruler with a scale of 1 to 10 on it. For me it's like a little sun inside my body that radiates light through my skin. It's like headlights on full beam when I'm at 10 (on an energy scale of 1–10) but sputters to a flicker barely discernible through my skin when I'm on, say, 2.

When you've found your metaphor, imagine your energy moving up the scale from 1 to 10. What would each stage look like?

Now imagine where you are right this moment. For me, it's 11 a.m. and, typing this, I'm on a 7. My interior sun is giving a steady, yellow glow, not flickering. This is good.

When I'm at 7, I can be pretty sure that I'll have the energy to accomplish the work I have to do today, cook dinner, whisk around doing a few chores and not be too irritable with my family. If I was on a 6, I might be a little worried. When I'm on 6 in the morning, it usually means I achieve nearly everything I have to do but I'm tired and irritable and snapping at the kids. Experience has taught me that there's no point in setting my alarm to get up early in the morning to do some work before the family arise, because I probably won't get out of bed and I'll feel angry at myself for not keeping to my plan. If I was on a 6, I'd be scaling down my work commitments for today and looking at how I could make the rest of the day easier for myself. Because if I do. I may be back on a 7 tomorrow; if I don't, there's a good chance I'll be on a 5 tomorrow – or worse.

Noting which people send your energy scale up or down is really useful. Then you can prepare for them. See IDEA 14, *Energy black holes*.

Try another idea…

The point of the energy scale is to help you recognise what's going on internally. When you drop below your own 7, it's time to absolutely prioritise one of your personal energy replenishers to restore your own vitality. And it only needs to be a short one. A half-hour comedy show, a bath, a glass of wine and a chat with some-one who makes you laugh.

'Most men pursue pleasure with such breathless haste that they hurry past it.'
SOREN KIERKEGAARD, philosopher

Defining idea…

123

Q   But what if you are just too busy when your level dips below 6?

A   *Let me show you why it saves you time in the end to stop and replenish your store of energy. You're right, of course. What often happens is that when people are really busy they start to cut down on the activities they see as superfluous to getting on with their job at hand. Guess what they are? Yes, the nourishing bath, the massage, sex, exercise. A delicious meal is foregone for a ready meal bunged in the microwave. But as you and I know, despite all our plans, when we're stressed we need to unwind, which is why we crack in periods of extreme busyness and end up in the pub, smoking our first fag in two years, or slumped in front of the TV, and oops, the whole bottle of wine is gone. The next day, when we need our energy again, we're several marks down on the energy scale.*

Q   My energy fluctuates between 3 and 8. What's going on?

A   *For the next two weeks, keep a diary. Check your energy scale three times a day: morning, afternoon and evening are good. Also note any times you consciously notice that you're tired or, conversely, brimming with energy. Make a note of the effect different people and situations or work activities have on your energy. Then you can do whatever you need to avoid or eliminate the energy drain, or replenish your energy to deal with it. For instance, I noticed that a particular piece of regular work that I do caused my energy levels to plummet. I didn't want to give it up though (although I considered it). Instead, I made sure I nurtured my energy levels every month in the week leading up to the energy drainer.*

28

Energy black spots transformed

Reframe your world. In even the most energy-draining situations, we can find a potential source of pep.

Some bits of the day just make us feel bad. Here's how to turn them around.

YOU HATE GETTING UP

Research has shown that pressing the snooze button doesn't actually make you less tired. An extra ten minutes – even an extra hour – doesn't refresh you. By getting up when you wake up, you reclaim time – and that is energising. Incapable of getting up? Instead of pressing the snooze button, try stretching. Think of a cat. Many animals have a good stretch before they rise to get their muscles stretched and warmed up and get oxygen into their blood stream. It will work for you too.

YOU HATE YOUR COMMUTE

See your commute as a chance to really get moving. There is nearly always some way you can make your commute to work more active. Walk to work. Or get off a stop early and walk a little of the way to work. Or walk up the escalator. Or walk up some of the stairs to your office. This will underline to your psyche that you are an active person, pursuing your vision of your future, energetically and dynamically. Play your own music on the way to work, if you don't already do so.

YOU HATE THE WAY YOUR WORKING DAY DISAPPEARS AND YOU FEEL YOU'VE ACHIEVED NOTHING

Use your lunch hour productively. Too many of us, even if we take a break from our desk, don't differentiate our lunch hour from the rest of the day when we're a wage slave. This hour is *your* hour. Make it a habit to do two things for yourself every lunch hour that will boost your energy – one you don't want to do, but will make your life easier, and one you do want to do, that will cheer you up. Make a phone call you're dreading, pay a bill, draft your CV – these are dull, but getting them off your list will make you feel better. Plan your next holiday, eat some chocolate, go for a walk – these are energising, and just for you. Reclaiming your lunch hour will mean every day has something positive in it.

YOU HATE WAITING

Here's an idea for you...

Eschew the lie-in. Research shows that catching up on sleep at the weekend knocks out your body clock and will lead to you being even more tired in the following week. As far as possible, go to bed and rise at the same time each day – it makes you less tired in the long run.

All those moments hanging around waiting at the check out, waiting for the train, or for the kettle to boil, or for the lift, can be put to use. Run over your goals and plans for the day. Think of the next challenge (whether that's a difficult phone call, exercising or facing someone you're not keen on). Run through the scene in your mind, imagining it going as well as possible and how you'll feel afterwards. 'Dead time' is usually filled with fantasies – often negative fantasies of all that could go wrong. Instead, start having positive fantasies that boost your confidence and energy. Or do some pelvic floor exercises – a toned pelvic floor means better orgasms for both sexes.

Go to IDEA 14, *Energy black holes*, for how to reframe your human energy drainers.

Try another idea…

YOU HATE BARBIE

Kids sap our energy by demanding attention, usually when we don't want to give it. The single best piece of advice is to give them that attention wholeheartedly. Becoming engaged in what children are interested in can be remarkably relaxing to the adult brain. Instead of begging for a couple of minutes to yourself to read the paper, help your child dress Barbie, complete their jigsaw or win at their computer game when they want you to do it. You'll find that two minutes of your attention will energise you and mean they are satisfied enough to leave you alone. The point is that if you have children you *do* have to spend time looking after them. So, personally, finding a way to make it relaxing and energising even when I'm overworked and stressed out really helps. When you're bathing the children, feeding them or dressing them, try to sink into their world, their level of interest, rather than having your mind racing with what's next on your agenda.

YOU HATE HANGOVERS

Nights out with friends are relaxing and essential, but have you noticed how rubbish you often feel the next day? A meal out, lots of booze, smoky atmospheres – no wonder. Suggest you see your friends in a different environment – a movie, a walk, a sauna or a night in a sushi bar (go easy on the sake) should make you feel better the next day rather than worse. If your friends like the pub and that's it, reduce your alcohol intake to one drink every second round.

'Regret is an appalling waste of energy. You can't build on it; it's only good for wallowing in.'
KATHERINE MANSFIELD, writer

Defining idea…

How did it go?

Q   I'm forcing myself out of bed. Why do I still feel awful?

A   *Throw out your dressing gown. Slobbing around in your PJs is great – for making you feel lethargic. Instead, lay your clothes out the night before and as soon as you roll out of bed, get straight into the shower. Then get dressed, put your shoes on and, if you're a woman (or indeed a man in touch with his feminine side – who am I to judge?), put on your make-up. When I was a new mother, I was given this tip and found it invaluable. I am a huge lover of my pyjamas but if I didn't get dressed right away, I would still be wandering around in them at 3pm, and it didn't feel luxurious, it felt seedy. Getting dressed confers a sense of purpose and get-up-and-go, and I recommend it especially to people who can spend a lot of day hanging around at home.*

Q   I don't see how playing with my children when I want to read the paper will energise me. Won't it just exhaust me more?

A   *An even better idea is to get them on your agenda. For example, you have to exercise? Take them to the park. They can bike or play football with you. You get the feel-good sensation of being a great parent. They see their parent modelling that exercise is a Good Thing. Top parenting, and you'll feel better, too. If you have a little work to do on the computer, set up a drawing centre for little children on the floor next to your desk loaded with pens, crayons and reams of paper. Often just being near you is enough to calm them down.*

29

The energy drench

Convert your shower into a daily spa treatment that will energise and revive you.

This will do you far more good than hitting the snooze button, or an extra cup of coffee. It will take about two minutes longer than your usual shower, but it does a whole lot more than get you clean.

ONE MINUTE? INVIGORATE YOUR SKIN BEFORE YOU GET IN THE SHOWER

Buy a natural-bristle skin brush – not so hard that it hurts your skin when you pass it over the back of your hand, but hard enough so that you feel it. Use this brush prior to showering. Brush over your skin, working from your feet up your legs, from your hands up your arms and over your back and torso, always working towards your heart. The theory is that this works to boost lymph flow, which means that waste products are eliminated from your body faster. There's no evidence for this. What is for sure is that it causes blood to flood the surface of the skin and thus

Give your insides an energy drench. Take a glass of hot water and squeeze a quarter of a lemon into it. Sip first thing. This supports your liver in expelling the waste that it's been working on processing all night.

increases circulation. It takes about a minute and it acts as a powerful tonic.

30 SECONDS? RUB AWAY THE OLD, REVEAL THE NEW

Continue to stimulate your system with a body scrub using a sisal glove or a face cloth. Plain old soap will do but a cleansing scrub scented with a citrus scent will wake you up even more. You can make your own scrub with a handful of coarse-grain salt to which you add a few drops of lemon, grapefruit or bergamot essential oil. Put some on your glove or cloth and rub your body vigorously. This action will get rid of the dead skin cells, softening your skin and invigorating you at the same time.

TWO MINUTES? DRENCH YOUR BODY

Turn on the tap and wash away your scrub with some warm water. Then change the temperature gauge to cool. Quite cool. And stay there for one minute. Return to hot again for a minute or so, and then back to cool for a final minute. The shock of passing between warm and cool will also boost your circulation. The capillary walls (those of the smallest blood vessels) are strengthened and skin tone is improved. You should feel as if you've run about half a mile by now.

30 SECONDS? CARRY ON THE GOOD WORK ALL DAY

Finally, 'mist' your body with oil. Make your own 'mister' by purchasing a spray bottle from a chemist, or recycling one that used to contain another product and has been washed out. For each 100ml of water, add half a teaspoon of olive or almond oil and ten drops of an energising oil. Bergamot, lemon or rosemary are all good.

Combine this with IDEA 20, *Willpower – it's all you need,* **on building willpower.**

Try another idea...

AN EXTRA FOR THE TIMES YOU'RE WASHING YOUR HAIR ...

3 minutes – get more focus

Rosemary essential oil is fabulous for restoring focus and energy. Wash your hair as normal, towel dry then use rosemary to lift your mood. If your hair is short, add three drops of rosemary essential oil to a couple of dessertspoons of almond oil and rub into your scalp. If your hair's long, add the oils to some conditioner and work into your hair. Now massage your scalp all over. Stick on a plastic hat or towel and follow the energy drench described above. When you've drenched your body, drench your hair and shampoo and condition again to get rid of the oils.

... AND FOR THOSE TIMES WHEN YOU FANCY A BATH

To maximise the restorative power of a bath at the end of the day, add one or two of drops of blue or green food colouring to your bath water along with your favourite bubble bath. Blue and green work powerfully on your brain to relax and calm you. Just a hint of green especially is very soothing. *Don't* overdo the colouring though.

'Energy is the essence of life. Every day you decide how you're going to use it by knowing what you want and what it takes to reach that goal, and by maintaining focus.'

OPRAH WINFREY

Defining idea...

131

Q   How can I go to work dripping with oil?

A   *That's the point of the mister. The small amount of oil means that the mist will cling to your skin and the fragrance will stay with you. By using a mister you don't end up too oily – not pleasant when you have to get dressed for work. But if it's not for you, add a few drops of oil to your usual body lotion.*

Q   I'm a bath person. Do I have to shower?

A   *I used to be one too, until I realised that it was my rubbish shower that I didn't like. You don't have to stick with it; for very little expense you can get a decent showerhead fitted onto your present system. A powerful shower is far more energising than any bath, but a bath will do as long as you don't spend too long in it. The idea of the drench is that it's short and sharp and brings a sense of urgency to your morning.*

30

What kind of time traveller are you?

Are you a P or a J? Finding out will turn your life around.

There are two main ways that human beings relate to time. Finding out yours could re-energise every aspect of your life, with no effort whatsoever.

Everyone's heard of Carl Jung, but few people realise the extent to which his ideas are still influencing us today. One of Jung's big ideas was to identify four pairs of 'preferences' – ways that human beings organise their world. A mother-daughter team of psychologists – Myers and Briggs – developed his ideas and Myers-Briggs theory was born. If you've applied for a job with a corporation, there's a good chance you've taken one of their tests of personality. Understanding where you fall in one of the preference pairs – what's known as the J-P dichotomy – could boost your energy by helping you understand how you use deadlines.

I won't bore you with what J and P stand for – it's irrelevant. What you need to know is that Js like things to be organised. It's essential for them to regulate and manage their lives. The want to reach decisions, get closure, move on. They need a plan, they

Here's an idea for you... **A quick test to find out whether you're P or J. Design a poster advertising an upcoming event. If you're a typical J, the date and time will feature strongly. If you're a typical P, you may have forgotten to mention them at all!**

need a timetable to achieve the plan and they need to be able to get on with the plan. If you are a J, your energy will be leached away if you're not allowed to follow your plan – usually by your P boss who won't sign off on it.

Ps value spontaneity and flexibility over organisation. They need the freedom to go with the flow. For example, they may plan to work all day and then when offered an invitation to lunch, accept it. Then they may well work doubly hard through the morning to make up time. Or they may not and miss their deadline. They'd rather experience life than control it and they feel confined by plans and definite commitments. They are energised by their resourcefulness in adapting to the demands of the moment.

You probably know if you're P or J by now, but if not, get a piece of paper and pen and write for a minute the answer to this question: What is really important about plans and planning?

If you're a typical J, you will have tackled the question with enthusiasm. If you're a typical P, your feelings will have ranged from slight feelings of dread and resistance to complete boredom.

HOW DOES UNDERSTANDING YOUR ATTITUDE TO TIME AFFECT YOUR ENERGY LEVELS?

Js need a lot of stamina. You'll worry about projects in advance, and although Ps seem to work harder right at the end to finish a project, you'll probably spend more hours on it because you'll set aside time and the job will expand to fill the hours.

You need to exercise, eat well, sleep and do all you can to support yourself on the long haul, especially if your boss is a P because they will drive you mad by refusing to follow a plan.

Go to IDEA 46, *Where do you go for energy?*, for more Jungian ideas to grow your energy levels.

Try another idea...

Ps, no matter how you buck against it, would benefit from a little bit of preparation each day, weeks in advance of a deadline. You will still leave significant amounts until the last minute because that's how you work best, but at least the ground-work will be done. In extreme cases Ps just don't 'see' deadlines anymore, but other people do and that's very stressful. Also, don't beat yourself up for being lazy because you work in fits and starts. The times Ps 'goof off' are just as vital as the times they work intensely.

HELL IS OTHER PEOPLE

Another point worth making. Both groups often profoundly mistrust the other group's way of working. Js think Ps disorganised and simply making life more complicated than it needs to be; Ps think Js anal and missing out on the best bits of life. Take a minute to dwell on whether your colleagues and, most importantly, your boss are likely to be Js or Ps. How much energy are you expending in placating groups that are the opposite of yours? One P friend of mine transformed her working life by throwing a sop to her J boss. She started showing her complex schedules and plans of work. She continued to work in the same haphazard way, but her boss's attitude to her was transformed. It was a win-win because my friend was more autonomous and her boss felt there was some control.

'There is no pleasure in having nothing to do; the fun is in having lots to do and not doing it.'

MARY WILSON LITTLE,
American writer
(She was a P if ever there was one.
If this quote irritates you, you're
definitely a J)

Defining idea...

135

How did
it go?

Q   I seem to be a bit of both. Is this normal?

A   *It's a scale: we're one or the other, but some people are more of a mixture, others more extreme. It's also entirely possible to be a P who has trained her self to be more J. That's what I've done since I've had children. Alternatively, Js train themselves to be more P so that they can enjoy the fruits of spontaneity and hanging out and being in the 'moment'.*

Q   I'm a P and I don't see what I've got to gain energy wise from being more J. Compared to Js I know, I'm positively dynamic. Aren't I better off as a P?

A   *One group is no better than the other. Both groups produce equally good work. The last-minute approach often prompts Ps to a surge of creative energy at the end, which is probably what you are referring to when you say Js may not seem as energetic as Ps – they're the tortoise to your hare. But that's just an assumption. However, there is some evidence, although it may be flawed, that Js actually live longer than Ps. Perhaps the sure and steady approach causes less stress to the system than a life time of adrenaline-fuelled achievement.*

31

Stop dithering, start living

Here's how to make swift, smart decisions.

Learn this vital decision-making formula. You'll free up your mind from niggling worries in seconds, saving your mental energy.

I've had a bit of a dilemma today. I'm staring at an e-mail advertising a two-day self-development course that I'd love to attend. There's just one problem. The weekend in question is the one (of admittedly many!) on which we will be celebrating my partner's fortieth birthday. I've promised to take him out for dinner that night and since the course is near my home, I could do both – attend the course during the day and take him for dinner that night. But … but … I've got that sneaking suspicion that by trying to pack too much in, I'm taking too much on. I'll be rushed and late for dinner.

In the past, this is the sort of dilemma I would have spent time on. I would have weighed up the pros and cons, written lists, talked to my partner about it, talked to friends perhaps, spent valuable time dithering when I could have been getting on with my life.

Here's an idea for you...

The very quickest form of this idea is brilliant for procrastinators. Think of a task that you're putting off. Imagine what the consequences will be in one month (or whatever time span is relevant) if you *don't* act. If the consequences don't frighten you, go to the pub; if they do, get on with it now. Worrying about it even subconsciously is sapping your energy.

But that was before I learned the magical qualities of what I call 'the power of 10' question.

When faced with any dilemma simply stop and ask yourself: what will the consequences be in:

10 minutes?
10 months?
10 years?

When you're faced with a problem where there's no win-win situation and someone will end up unhappy, at least in the short term, 'the power of 10' helps you cut through the emotions of the moment and focus on what is really important.

Let's take my present dilemma.

If I decide to go to the self-development course, what will be the repercussions in 10 minutes? None. I'll explain to my partner, he won't really register it – it's down the line and as long as I'm not actually cancelling dinner, he won't care. I'll be happy.

In 10 months? That depends. If there are no mess-ups and I get there on time, probably it will be fine. But if I am late for dinner, in 10 months' time, he'll still be making sarcastic comments.

In 10 years? You know, that's the tricky one. Even if I manage everything, I think he's still going to remember that on the weekend of his fortieth, I wasn't really around. That's the general impression he'll have long after he's forgotten the presents, the party and all the other gestures I'll make to 'big' up his birthday and distract his attention from the fact that I'm not actually there very much. Would I be better off attending the course? I might learn a lot. I might make some lifelong soulmates. But there's no way of knowing if it will be worth it, or not. And there's potentially a lot to lose. So this time, I think I'll have to pass.

If dithering is affecting your sleep, see IDEA 6, *How to get enough sleep.*

Try another idea...

It took me as long to make that decision as it took to type it, and now my mind is free to get on with writing this, and everything else I have to do. I won't waste any more time thinking about it.

This is a variation of an old idea – imagining yourself one year, five years, ten years down the road is commonplace. 'What will it matter in twenty years' time?' we say to each other. But I find 'the power of 10' particularly elegant and easy to use. Try it when you're not sure what route to take and know that either will end up making someone unhappy. The three different timescales help you see through the emotional turmoil of yours or somebody else's short-term unhappiness to what the potential benefits could be when disappointment has passed. It helps you cut through the emotional 'fuss' that occurs when your plans are unpopular with some people, and to see clearly if they're worth the grief.

'But all will be well, and every kind of thing will be well.'
JULIAN OF NORWICH.
Medieval mystic

Defining idea...

**Q None of us know what's going to happen in ten years, so isn't
this all a bit pointless?**

A *Imagining yourself ten years down the line helps highlight what might be
make-or-break moments in your life. For instance, with the example above,
I realised that if this was my partner's thirty-ninth birthday, I would probably have behaved differently. If it was just any old birthday of my partner's, I might choose to go to the weekend training. But the fact that it's
his fortieth birthday – a memorable, important one – changes my view.*

**Q I did a version of this idea when I made the decision to go part-
time so I could spend some more time with my children. But I'm
pretty miserable at work now, and pretty miserable at home.
What went wrong?**

A *I'm assuming that you wanted to spend more time with your children and
that you felt that in ten years' time you would regret it if you didn't, no
matter what the financial or career repercussions now. Remember that.
Your view probably hasn't changed. But unfortunately, this idea doesn't
guarantee that you'll be happy. You may still have quite a bit of work to
do to form your life into something that works. Do 'the power of 10' again
with this question: 'If I was at home with the children all the time, how
would it be?' And another question: 'If I had a different job, one I loved,
how would I feel in 10 minutes, 10 months, 10 years?' Keep playing around
with the question until you isolate the source of unhappiness in your life.
Then you can change it.*

32

Get in the raw

Eating more raw food – we're talking carrots rather than chicken – is a well-documented route to raising energy levels.

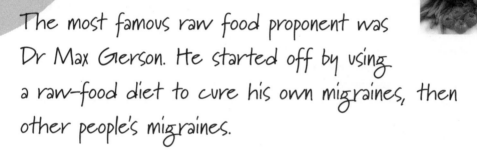

The most famous raw food proponent was Dr Max Gerson. He started off by using a raw-food diet to cure his own migraines, then other people's migraines.

Then he moved on 'up' the disease ladder until he became famous for his treatment of cancer. Gerson believed that the starting point of all illness is an imbalance between sodium and potassium. His theory was that eating raw fruit and veg (which are loaded with potassium) increases oxygen uptake by the cells and mobilises white blood cells to fight disease. This results in better health and vastly improved energy.

Most doctors wouldn't agree with this, but then they wouldn't disagree that, as a nation, we'd benefit from upping our fruit and vegetable consumptions. Personally, I once followed a 100% raw food diet for a month and felt marvellous on it after just

Here's an idea for you...

What puts people off juicing is that the preparation and clean-up after takes longer than drinking the juice. The secret is to gather all the ingredients of your juice together and fill your sink with soapy water before you start. Chop and clean in one shot. When the juice is made, pop the dirty bits straight into hot water to soak while you sip your juice slowly. Soaking immediately makes clearing up much quicker.

a few days. I had energy to burn and seemed to achieve much more completely effortlessly. But it is a huge faff at first and can take over your life. I once read a fascinating account by a journalist of living on raw juices for a few weeks in an attempt to reverse the genetic condition that would mean she'd be blind in her thirties. To her amazement, and that of her ophthalmologist, her sight improved during her experiment, but she found the effort of juicing vast quantities of vegetables every day too high a price to pay. She couldn't leave her home, shackled as she was to her juicer.

The writer and alternative-health guru, Leslie Kenton, is a devotee of raw food. Her realistic recommendation is for a diet that is 75% raw and 25% good-quality cooked wholegrains (brown rice, wholemeal, organic bread). At this level of raw food intake, she believes you get all the health benefits, including an increase in vitality. She has written extensively on how to transfer to a raw-food diet.

You would have to be very motivated to move over onto even a 75% raw-food diet. Another option is to gradually introduce more raw foods into your normal diet. What you will probably find is that, as you eat more raw food, you will enjoy the 'clean' taste and find that you are gradually including more healthy, less processed foods. It goes without saying that the gurus of raw food insist on organic:

where that's not possible, scrub all produce thoroughly under running water.

SOME IDEAS THAT ARE EASY TO INSTIGATE

Turn to IDEA 3, *How to eat*, for more about the best foods for energy and combine it with this one.

Try another idea...

- Eat a bowl of salad leaves a day – rocket, lettuce, basil, parsley, watercress. Experiment with different types. Grate a little carrot or apple over your leaves, or add some homemade vinaigrette, balsamic vinegar or olive oil.
- Start every meal with raw food. For breakfast, fruit; for lunch, fruit or a salad; for dinner, salad again. It is an easy way to up your five fruit and veg, and as a side effect it should help you lose weight: research showed that those who ate a small salad before dinner ate less at the meal and lost weight effortlessly.
- Buy a juicer. Vegetable and fruit juices give a concentrated shot of vitamins and minerals, and they are easily digested. Recent research shows that drinking fruit and vegetable juice three times a week slashes the risk of Alzheimer's disease by 76%. (The Gerson Diet, incidentally, recommends ten huge glasses a day.)
- Make your own coleslaw. One of the very easiest ways of including more raw food is to grate half a cabbage, a couple of carrots and an apple into a bowl and mix up with a minimal amount of mayonnaise. Or better still, skip the mayonnaise and soften the slaw with your own homemade vinaigrette sweetened with a little honey. This tastes so good that commercial coleslaws will soon seem too cloying.

'Everyone has a doctor in him or her; we just have to help it in its work. The natural healing force within each one of us is the greatest force in getting well. Our food should be our medicine. Our medicine should be our food.'

HIPPOCRATES

Defining idea...

How did it go?

Q **But isn't it healthier to eat the whole fruit or vegetable rather than juice?**

A *Replacing all fruit and vegetables with juice is a mistake because your body needs fibre (not least to control cholesterol levels) and the fibre is reduced in juices. But raw fruit and veg is very good for you because the nutrients have not been dissipated by the cooking process, and juicing is an easy way of getting raw food, especially in winter when salads aren't so alluring. I find the recipes in Jason Vale's books and website inspiring. During the summer I make this version of his Salad in a Glass most days (you can find the original on his website): 1 stick celery; 1 tomato; 1/4 cucumber; hand-ful of salad leaves; 1 carrot; 1 apple, ¼ teaspoon of grated ginger. Juice up and add ice.*

Q **If I just eat fruit during the day, and my normal evening meal, won't that give me the 75:25 ratio?**

A *Eating only fruit won't give you energy during the day. The odd one-day fruit fast – eating just apples or just grapes – is a reasonable energy booster when you don't have much on. Many people find giving their system a rest from difficult-to-digest foods is an easy way of feeling better. But fruit is like any other carbohydrate: it gives you a sharp-ish rise in blood sugar followed by a hunger for something more substantial pretty soon. It's just got much more going for it nutrition-wise than a biscuit, but on a daily basis, you need to eat more than fruit to be energetic.*

33

Beware crash and burn

A recent study from the University of Helsinki confirms that burnout is far more common than previously thought, particularly in staff who are overworked.

And these days that's just about anyone in a job.

One textbook definition of burnout is 'a state of fatigue and frustration due to devotion to a way of life that does not produce the expected reward'. The 'way of life' can be a relationship – it doesn't have to be a job.

As academic researchers have pinpointed, burnout is more likely when reward does not meet expectation, and 'reward' doesn't refer merely to money. We associate burnout with jobs like banking and law, but those with a huge salary don't have a monopoly. The highest rates of burnout are amongst teachers and primary health-care workers. People who are idealistic, who want to help, who keep on giving without looking after themselves – these are prime candidates for burnout.

ARE YOU BURNING OUT?

The best book I've found on the subject of burnout is Dr Dina Glouberman's *The Joy of Burnout*. She went through burnout herself and, according to her, these are some of the classic symptoms:

- extreme tiredness
- inability to relax
- emotional deadness
- chronic anger
- loss of appetite for food, sex, life
- poor attention
- speeding up without increased effectiveness
- an increase in watching TV, drinking, eating junk food, shopping, casual sex, using internet chat rooms accompanied by closing off from family and friends/colleagues.

If you have no energy coupled with a lack of interest and enjoyment in life, take action immediately to accept that there is a problem. Ignoring the problem could lead to a

Here's an idea for you...

Take this quick quiz. So: 'It's important that I'm always seen to "hold it together"'; 'Helping others is reward enough, even if they don't seem to appreciate it'; 'My full effort is needed if anything is to be achieved'. Do these sentences resonate with you? They are the sorts of ideas that perfectionists accept without question. Perfectionists are more prone to burnout. If you believe in just one of these sentences, you should take extra care.

complete loss of energy, so much so that you cannot carry on working. The symptoms are similar to those of depression; but with depression, symptoms can continue for all of your life; with burnout, eventually there is a collapse and sufferers have to spend a great

Read IDEA 7, Are you confusing energy with adrenaline? Overdrive is often a stage on the way to burnout.

Try another idea...

deal of time in bed with symptoms that look very like ME. The aim is to stop the rot before it gets to that stage – that might mean drastic action such as taking leave from work, or a temporary break from a relationship.

Burnout is also characterised by a loss of love for the life we have led, even if we have struggled really hard to build that life.

'Burnout is not just about having a "big job" or being very busy,' says Hermione Elliot, a therapist who specialises in treating it. 'It is about losing our idea of our-selves.' In other words, our way of life doesn't satisfy us anymore. It is a crisis of spirit as much as a physical breakdown. This is very hard; often we know that we are unhappy but changing the situation means giving up our way of life, and that can often seem impossible. Try not to panic. Take steps to help your body recover from fatigue and be patient: a solution to your problem will eventually become clear. The important thing is to accept that there *is* a problem. Pretending everything is fine, when you secretly know that it is not, will ultimately be unproductive.

'**Burnout is the state of mind ... reached by those who have come to the end of a particular road but haven't acknowledged this ... it can be a door to ... a life of joy ... a sense of being able to be one's true self.'**

DR DINA GLOUBERMAN, *The Joy of Burnout*

Defining idea...

1   *Look after yourself.* Self-care is essential. Eating healthily and taking time out for yourself to walk or do yoga, or some other method of moving your body that appeals to you, will help you get balance.

2   *Enter the zone.* Burnout is characterised by an inability to relax. Rituals, establishing 'comfort zones' where you can relax and switch off, are easy ways of turning off your brain. This could be listening to a piece of music you love when you come home from work, meditating at lunchtime, having a bath each morning – time for yourself at the same time every day that you can look forward to without fail.

3   *Be quiet long enough to listen.* Your body will be sending you messages other than loss of energy – for instance, unexplained aches and pains, or repeated infections. The easy route is to ignore these messages and keep rushing around in an effort to ignore what you know is wrong. Remember that it takes courage just to listen to the voice, let alone act on it, so don't be hard on yourself. However, there is no 'sticking plaster' approach that will work: eventually, your body will need to escape from the stress that it's under, by getting sick if necessary.

Q   **I am tired, but I don't sound as ill as people with total burnout.**
       Have I got it or not?

How did it go?

A   *Do these statements resonate?*
- *I don't enjoy my work any longer*
- *Time with family and friends feels like one more chore*
- *I feel I'm doing more and more but getting nowhere*
- *I'm not doing as much as I could*
- *If I don't do it, no one will, but I don't know how long I can go on*
- *I feel trapped*
- *I feel isolated and alone*
- *I'm not as effective as I used to be*

If any of them sound familiar, you could use some time out to work out what sort of life you would like to lead. Allow your imagination to run riot – what would a perfect life look like to you? And try hard to let those who love you know what you are going through. This can be very hard for them, but cutting them off won't help.

Q   **Is this just another word for a mid-life crisis?**

A   *It can be, but it's bleaker than that. Mid-life crisis is a bit of a joke. There's nothing funny about burnout. We're still trying to maintain our old life-style, but it's not who we are any longer. And when we realise that we've been expending all this energy in the wrong direction, it hits us as hard as a bereavement. It is profoundly painful. Also, burnout is hitting people at an ever-younger age, probably because of the pressure on young people to have it all – and all of it 'perfect'.*

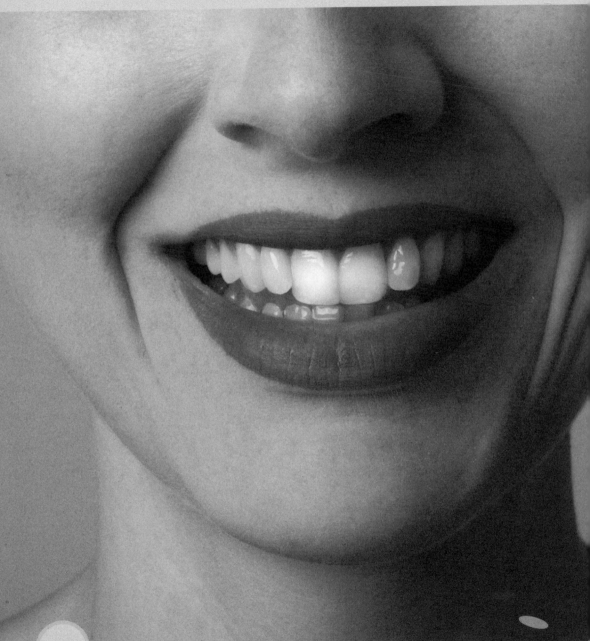

34

Are you getting enough?

Pleasure is what we're talking about. Jumping off the hamster wheel of relentless grind energises you very fast indeed.

Fruit, vegetables, exercise — we all know that they improve well being. But the part of the equation that science is just waking up to is pleasure.

Here's a fact: people who enjoy life live a longer, healthier life. The research into why happy *bons viveurs* live longer, in better health, is still in its infancy, but we're learning more every day.

One of the pioneers in what is called 'positive psychology' was a Yugoslav psychologist by the name of Dr Grossarth-Maticek, who did some studies into 3000 elderly Germans. He measured how often they felt pleasure and then followed them up twenty-one years later. The results showed that the 300 with the highest score (who had the most pleasure) were thirty times more likely to be alive, healthy and happy compared with the 200 with the lowest score.

Here's an idea for you...

Make a list of the activities you used to love when you were around 17 or 18 years old – a pretty sure sign of what the 'real you' really loves. You're looking for a minimum of ten activities. Pick one and carve out the time to do it in the next week. Work your way through the list of activities that still appeal.

The author of *The Attitude Factor*, Thomas R Blakeslee, has done a lot to publicise this research. 'Many people think [pleasure] is a luxury,' he wrote, ' but it's a vital necessity for good health and long life.'

Blakeslee took the theory further. He reckoned that at around thirty years old, we start to close down to pleasure, partly because we shut out new experiences and are less interested in new things. Basically we allow our ability to be adventurous to atrophy – and that directly impacts on how much pleasure there is in our lives. We stay in our comfort zone, and that comfort zone gets smaller and smaller.

Who cares, you might well be thinking (perhaps a tad defensively)? Who cares if my idea of excitement is a new series of *Celebrity Big Brother*? Big deal. Well, it is actually. If you're a couch potato, you are literally killing yourself. Traditional medics would say that it's because you're getting no exercise. Blakeslee would say it's because you're boring yourself to death.

To get you thinking, this is my much-simplified version of the quiz first given to the Germans and explained in full in Blakeslee's book and on his website. Base your answers on your usual behaviour and feelings in the last year, and pick the answer than is closest for you, even if not absolutely right. Add up your score from the bracketed figures.

Defining idea...

Life is full of misery, loneliness, suffering unhappiness, and it's all over much too quickly.'
WOODY ALLEN

1   Imagine you wake up on a beautiful summer morning without a care in the world. You feel happy. How happy?
       Slightly (score 1) Moderately (4) Intensely (7)

2   How long do these feelings last?
       Seconds (1) Hours (4) All day (7)

3   How often do you take pleasure in simple things such as a good meal or a conversation with a friend?
       Almost never (1) Weekly (4) Every day (7)

4   Look at your diary. How many events have you scheduled for the future that are guaranteed to give you pleasure?
       None (1) One or two (4) Plenty (7)

5   When you think of the future, how sure are you that you're going to have sensations of sheer pleasure in the future?
       Not at all (1) Pretty sure (4) Certain (7)

6   Think about the greatest pleasure you've ever had in your life. Do you think you'll feel that much pleasure again?
       Unlikely (1) Perhaps (4) Sure (7)

7   When you feel that all is well with the world, how strongly do you feel it?
       Minimally (1) Moderately (4) Intensely (7)

8   How often do you experience this kind of feeling of wellbeing?
       Almost never (1) Weekly (4) Many times in a week (7)

9   Think of the best you've ever felt in yourself. Do you think you'll feel that good again?
       Unlikely (1) Perhaps (4) Sure (7)

10   After feelings of pleasure and wellbeing, do you get negative feelings such as guilt or depression?
       Almost always (1) Sometimes (4) Almost never (7)

Add up you score and divide by ten.

If you scored 1-4. Your pleasure quotient is low, and your chances of being healthy and well in 21 years, are according to this research lower unless you start planning for pleasure now.

If you scored 4.1 –6. This corresponds to the people who had a 45–55% chance of being healthy twenty-one years later. So pretty good, but could do better.

If you scored 6.1-7. Your score on this quiz corresponds to the people who had the most pleasure in their lives, and consequently the healthiest outcome on follow-up.

A TWO-PRONGED ATTACK IS NEEDED

- *Plan for pleasure.* Dedicate time every day to simply enjoying life and planning for fun. Knowing you have something to look forward to, rather than letting life just happen, is a wonderful energiser. Plan something pleasurable for tonight, next Wednesday night, and one weekend in the next six months, just for starters.
- *Bust out of the comfort zone.* Why is this so important? Because it's the simplest route to intense pleasure. Anything we have to work for, we appreciate more. Start a conversation with someone interesting in the lunch queue, go to a foreign-language movie, book up to go abseiling. It doesn't matter how much you actually enjoy these things; you'll feel great after doing them just because you pushed yourself.

Try another idea... **If you react strongly against this idea, or feel indifferent at the thought of more pleasure in your life, turn to IDEA 33, *Crash and burn*.**

Q   **The comfort zone hit home. But is making time for more reading**   *How did*
and more bubble baths (which give me pleasure) really going to   *it go?*
push my boundaries?

A   *It's a good start. No one's saying you have to take up parascending or bareback horse riding. Start with something easy but different. Think of the last time you were invited to try something new and you said 'no'. It doesn't need to be a direct invitation. Perhaps an author is reading his latest book at your local bookshop. Perhaps a new kind of takeaway has opened. Promise yourself for the next month, whenever you're asked to try something new, or your attention is caught by something different, you'll say 'yes' instead of 'no'.*

Q   **What if don't have time to do all the stuff I have to do already?**

A   *Schedule ten minutes a day to do something that you really love. Stick to it. Everyone has ten minutes.*

35

Eat breakfast

If you don't, you're missing out on the number one trick for combating energy loss.

I'm evangelical about this one. If you're tired, and you don't eat breakfast — that's probably the reason.

I'm not a person who likes to eat in the morning, but years of talking to nutritional experts brainwashed me. They all said it was vital. I started. My energy levels soared, specifically my mental focus. The difference in concentration is so fundamental that now, no matter how frantic my morning, I won't drive unless I've eaten breakfast.

This has turned me into a breakfast fascist. If I were an employer, I wouldn't care about the standard of a potential employee's CV if they wouldn't promise to eat breakfast each morning. They may not realise it, but they are certainly not performing to their full potential, even if they think they are.

The best fuel combination is a carbohydrate and protein breakfast. Carbohydrate releases energy quickly (it gives you the boost to run for the bus), but protein releases energy for longer (it will help you clinch the deal during that tricky pre-lunch conference call). If you eat carbs alone in the morning or nothing at all, your

Here's an idea for you... **Try this heart-boosting smoothie, which fulfils all the criteria. Mix half a pint of ice-cold semi-skimmed or soya milk with a banana, a pinch of cinnamon and two teaspoons of fish or flaxseed oil. Throw in a handful of soft fruits such as raspberries, blueberries or strawberries. (Out of season, you can buy frozen packets of these in supermarkets.) Sip, with a handful of nuts.**

body may well crave more carbs at 11 a.m. – hence the dreaded doughnut run that wreaks such havoc with your figure and your idea of yourself as a person in control of their life. So remember. Carbs good, bit of protein essential. Here are some ideas:

OK BREAKFAST

Bowl of non-sugary cereal (Shreddies, All-Bran) with semi-skimmed or skimmed milk. Piece of fruit or good-quality juice.

How to make it better

The milk provides some protein, but not much. Nibble on a little hard cheese or cottage cheese, or have a slice of cheese on wholewheat toast to get some more protein in there.

BETTER BREAKFAST

Porridge with plain yogurt and a handful of seeds and dried fruit and/or a teaspoon of honey to sweeten.

How to make it better

Again, try the cheese thing, or a handful of nuts on top of the porridge. You may find that the yogurt does enough to fill you up. It does sometimes for me. But not always. Which is why you should build up to the ...

BEST BREAKFAST

- Scrambled eggs on wholegrain toast.
- Mackerel or kippers on wholegrain toast.
- Smoked salmon and cream cheese on wholegrain toast or bagel.
- Omelette with cheese, tomato and mushrooms.

How to make it better

Add a piece of fruit and you're set to go.

MY FAVOURITE BREAKFAST

My friend Lynn Osborne, a gifted acupuncturist, gave me two nutritional tips – green tea and drinking chicken soup for breakfast. A bowl of homemade chicken soup is a marvellous breakfast on a cold morning – on any morning. Protein, vegetables (for carbohydrate) and filling without being fattening. You can throw in some noodles if you feel like it. You feel light and full of energy. Use your own recipe or try this one. This makes enough for five bowls. Keep half in the fridge and freeze the other half until later on in the week.

Any protein/carbohydrate combo will work. Turn to **IDEA 42, *Supermarket savvy,*** for some inspiration on superfoods.

Try another idea...

'*To eat well in England, you should have breakfast three times a day.*'
SOMERSET MAUGHAM

Defining idea...

Buy yourself a special breakfast bowl. Enjoy your soup as you drink it. Think of China – calm and peace (which is, of course, where Lynn picked up the habit during her training).

Sauté one chopped leek and one chopped onion in a little olive oil, then add a minced garlic clove and cook until they are transparent. Add three chopped potatoes, one chopped carrot and 1¼ litres of chicken or vegetable stock, plus a handful or two of cooked, shredded organic chicken. Throw in a pinch of nutmeg, grated ginger or horseradish if you like. Bring to the boil and then turn down the heat and simmer for fifteen minutes or until the potatoes are cooked. Add a handful of greens – pak choi, spinach leaves, curly kale, watercress – and continue to simmer until these are just cooked. I like mine chunky but you could liquidise yours if you prefer. Add pepper. I don't use salt, and if you do, try to cut down.

Q   **I've got no time, no inclination – and you really expect me to face this?**

How did it go?

A   *Investigate ways to make shakes using whey protein from healthfood shops palatable. These are pure protein, usually used by body builders to maximise their protein intake without eating half a cow a day. You take a scoop, add some juice, milk or water, and blend it. You can add some fruit to make it more palatable. I've also heard good things about Get Up & Go! Powder: mixed with half a pint of milk and a banana, it gives you 100% of your RDA of every vitamin and mineral, with that all-important protein and carbohydrate combination. Personally, these aren't for me – I like food as real as possible, but it does satisfy the criteria.*
    It takes five minutes. You've got five minutes.

Q   **No. I don't. What else?**

A   *Will keeping you slim act as an incentive? Eating breakfast, according to Harvard Medical School, reduces your chances of being overweight by one third, but it also makes you 50% less likely to have blood-sugar problems. Now we have to have some tough love and talk priorities. Eating breakfast will give you energy. Eat the wrong thing for breakfast and you risk an energy crash mid-morning, but any breakfast is better than no breakfast. Start with a croissant or an energy bar (usually not much better for you than a chocolate bar). Or indeed, have a chocolate bar. But have something.*

36

Let in the light

Most of us have heard of SAD – Seasonal Affective Disorder – but are less aware that there are millions of people affected by the 'sub-syndrome'.

They don't have SAD, but they feel exhausted all winter.

Before electricity, everything changed for our ancestors during the winter months. Lack of daylight affected every part of their lives. Now we can work and play round the clock; the lack of light need never impinge on our 'lifestyle'.

But that doesn't mean that lack of daylight doesn't have a profound effect on us.

Normal electric lights can't replace daylight as far as our bodies are concerned, which explains why millions of us suffer symptoms of SAD unwittingly. And lack of energy is one of the biggest symptoms.

Around one in twenty of us suffer from SAD, which can involve severe depression. But what's amazing is that so many of us don't realise it and a far, far larger number are believed by experts to suffer from a milder form without ever knowing it. And lack of energy is the clearest symptom of this 'sub-syndrome'.

- Do you dread the winter months?
- Do you feel lethargic during the months of November to April for no apparent reason?

Here's an idea for you... **Have your morning cuppa outside if at all possible, or next to a bright window. Research on sheep in the Western Isles has led scientists to believe that SAD is related to levels of melatonin, the hormone that induces sleep. We need daylight to 'switch off' melatonin after a night's sleep, and getting outside as soon after you wake (as long as it's light, of course) may help.**

- Do you tend to put on weight in winter?
- Do you find it near impossible to get out of bed in the morning when it's dark outside?
- Do you find you are more paranoid or self-doubting in winter?
- Do you feel more anxious in winter?

Answer yes to two or more and there's every chance you could be affected by SAD.

The further north you live, the more likely you are to be affected by the lack of light. One study has shown that those in the north-east of Scotland have a higher level of SAD symptoms than average, and it is likely that depression in winter gets gradually more likely the farther north you live, as the light available diminishes.

WHAT CAN YOU DO?

Stage 1

Get outside for half an hour a day during the winter. Make it a habit of going for a walk at lunchtime, but since sunlight is so precious in the UK during winter, if at all possible, think about dropping everything, making your excuses and getting outside as soon as the sun comes out, whatever time of the day.

Stage 2

If you still feel blue, St John's Wort has been proven to help with the symptoms of SAD. It is not suitable for those on some other medications including the Pill and some heart drugs.
It is also helpful in combating the comfort eating that goes along with mild depression.

> Using colour as well as light will help boost your energy. See IDEA 41, *Colour your life energetic.*

Try another idea...

Stage 3

Investing in a light box, which supplies doses of strong white light as you work, or sit in your home, could well be answer. A study published in the *American Journal of Psychiatry* found that light therapy was more effective than Prozac in treating SAD: 95% of its users reported that it improved their condition. In general, 85% appear to benefit from light boxes and see an improvement within three to four days of treatment of around two hours a day. Specialised light boxes can be found on the internet, but lights are now readily available on your high street, at chemists and health shops. For milder cases there are 'alarm clocks' that wake you gently and gradually in the morning with light rather than ringing.

> '*Do not anticipate trouble, or worry about what may never happen. Keep in the sunlight.*'
> BENJAMIN FRANKLIN

Defining idea...

Stage 4

If depression is a problem, the group of anti-depressants that work best are the SSRIs (Selective Serotonin Reuptake Inhibitors).

Older kinds such as the tri-cyclics tend to make you feel more lethargic and tired, so they aren't the best option if you are already tired.

How did it go?

Q **I think I may have it because I'm so tired in winter but I don't feel depressed. Doesn't SAD always make you depressed?**

A *SAD is characterised by depression but when it is absent and exhaustion is more of a problem, it is known as sub-syndrome. This makes it likely that you are one of the people not recognised to have SAD. Overeating is also common in the sub-syndrome, but depression and anxiety not so much.*

Q **Can I get a light box on the NHS?**

A *No. They aren't cheap but they do start at under £100 now, and VAT has been removed on them, which is something. You do see results quickly and there are ways of trialling them to see if they'll work for you. Check out self-help websites such as www.sada.org.uk.*

37

Liberate endorphins

A psychologist called Maslow first came up with what's now known as the Maslow Hierarchy. His big idea is that human beings have an inherent desire to satisfy some core needs. Then we can worry about our energy levels.

Until people's basic needs are satisfied, they can't concentrate on anything else. Once satisfied, they can use their energy for other things — like self-fulfilment.

Basically you, me and everyone else we know has to have enough food and water; shelter and warmth; in other words, physical security before we can start thinking of the finer things in life.

The reason I think this is so important is that although practically all of us in the Western, developed, rich world appear to have our core needs satisfied, we don't feel safe. We have physical security yet we feel increasingly insecure. And feeling unsafe takes a lot of our energy. We fear having our social status and income taken away from us. We fear for our children. We fear old age.

Here's an idea for you...

When we're relaxed we breathe at between five and eight times a minute. Consciously bringing your breath down to that rate automatically calms you down, whatever else is going on. See the air you're breathing as liquid energy, revitalising your whole system.

The world did change on 9/11 – the biggest change is that people who never felt unsafe before are afraid every time they travel or even visit a big city. Climate change is another thing that worries us all. More choice and, let's face it, more wealth have been coupled with more insecurity.

There's no easy answer to this. The only method I can suggest for free-flowing anxiety is to learn how to feel safe on a day-to-day basis. I've written about what I called CAD – creeping anxiety disorder, that sense that life is gradually becoming ever more worrying. During research I interviewed William Bloom, who has some interesting answers to all sorts of big questions, and specifically on feeling stronger in yourself. You can check his website on www.williambloom.com.

From his ideas, I have developed a quick way of feeling safe whenever and wherever I am. Practise this whenever you feel that fear and insecurity are draining your energy and taking your focus away from what you should be concentrating on.

PARENT YOURSELF

When you're feeling 'antsy', through stress, discomfort or tiredness, when you're stuck in a traffic jam, angry with our partner, feeling scared and fearful because you're sure you're being followed – think of your body as a distressed child and your mind as its loving parent. As a parent anchors a child by holding its hand, anchor your body by detaching your mind from your thoughts and what's going on around you and 'focus down' into your body. Try thinking of a spot in your belly below your navel and above your genital area, deep in your abdomen. Focusing down stops your brain from catastrophising, and thus switches off the release of adrenaline and cortisol.

Worry stops us making decisions. See IDEA 31, *Stop dithering, start living.*

Try another idea…

THINK BEAUTIFUL THOUGHTS

Remember something beautiful and good that you love. I find it helps whenever you have a spare moment to remember good times with people you love. It means you have a ready supply of good thoughts at the forefront of your brain, ready to call on when you're next stressed. Thinking good thoughts liberates endorphins, the feel-good opiate chemicals that are the basis of all happiness.

BREATHE DOWN

Relax. Take a deep breath and let it flow down into that spot in your belly.

By switching off the stress hormones, focusing on the positive, you're now calm and ready to expend your energy where it's needed – not on being scared.

'There is no safety in numbers, or in anything else.'
JAMES THURBER, American humourist

Defining idea…

169

How did it go?

Q **I'm feeling very insecure at the moment. My boss hates me, my girlfriend has left me and my friends are fed up with me moaning. Any other ideas?**

A   *Poor you. Despite the positive attitude that I try to maintain at all times, I do believe that there are times when, through no fault of our own, we become scapegoats. It's not our imagination. The world really is out to get us. All of us have to serve our time as scapegoat; look around and you'll see some immensely powerful people going through it right now. And those times make us feel very insecure. The question is, how to get through it? Try doing this twice a day, say, first thing in the morning and mid-afternoon. Imagine that you are surrounded by an impermeable bubble. Inside your bubble you are safe and well, and negative thoughts can't penetrate it. Some people find it helps to see their bubble as gold or pink. Or imagine that you are covered in shining, flexible, immensely strong armour.*

Q **But what about me inside the bubble? What if I still feel awful?**

A   *At the same time, when thoughts of your girlfriend or your boss permeate, concentrate on your breath and say 'I breathe in negativity, I breathe out love'. If this is all sounding a bit 'new age' for you, suspend disbelief. These tactics have worked for lots of clever people for centuries and they could well work for you too, given half a chance.*

38

Getting down and dirty

Say hello to your shadow side. A bit like your bank manager, he may not be terrific company, but you kind of need him around.

Ignoring him can drain your energy without you even realising why. PS: You're going to need your duster.

Maintaining free-flowing energy depends on maintaining balance – emotional, physical and spiritual. When it comes to spiritual, there is one very easy way of keeping everything yin and yang. Embracing your dark side.

What's this got to do with your energy levels? Stick with me.

Two famous Jungian psychotherapists, Dr Marie-Louise von Franz and Barbara Hannah, shared a house in Switzerland. When one of them had a piece of good luck, praise, acclaim or other good fortune, she was required to take out the bins for a week. This is seen in Jungian terms as 'playing out the shadow side' to balance the positive boost to your psyche. A simpler way of looking at it is 'keeping your feet on the ground'. It's one of those old-fashioned qualities we like to think we have naturally. But think about it. How grounded are you?

Here's an idea for you...

Becoming involved in recycling is a good way to get in touch with your shadow side. Whatever your political views as to how much good it does the planet, attempting to recycle absolutely everything cannot but help but make you focus very strongly on what you buy and what you waste. Don't limit yourself simply to paper – everything but raw protein can be recycled these days if you start making your own compost.

Now that so many of we ordinary people have prosperity our forebears could only dream of – for instance, enough to employ a cleaner where our grandmothers could never have afforded it – I wonder if we have lost touch with the bare bones of our lives: clearing up after ourselves. I'm prepared to believe that if we don't tend to our own lives but let someone else do it, we get somehow stuck. We are out of touch with our money ('sticking it on the plastic'), our homes (cleaners and labour-saving devices are commonplace), our responsibilities (we have accountants and financial advisers to make decisions for us), and sometimes, tragically, even our children. I only have to look at some of our favourite celebrities – people who haven't cleared up their own mess for a very long time – to see the effect it has on the psyche: delusion, unhappiness, dysfunction and in some cases, quite clearly, mental illness. If you don't clear up your rubbish – literally – pretty soon you're in a mess spiritually too.

The importance of getting down and dirty came home to me this summer. The best energy booster I know is to throw out your clutter and streamline your belongings so all you've got is what is beautiful and what is useful (and used, often!). I'm a mad de-clutterer. But recently, my standards slipped a bit. Six months ago, we moved into a house that is best described as a 'dump'. It has not been touched in 57 years. Except for where the previous owners tacked up bits of hardboard over the fireplaces, windows and doorways to keep out draughts (there was no heating or hot water). The paintwork is so dilapidated that, even after it's been scrubbed, it still looks dirty. No amount of spit and polish will make this house look good until, eventually, room by room we renovate it. We can't clear space because we need doors and bits of wood and MDF to be stored somewhere – in the hallway usually. Clutter became a way of life.

This isn't a call to get back in the kitchen. Check out IDEA 34, Are you getting enough? to make sure you have a balance.

Try another idea...

And I got tired. Really tired. Then I remembered about celebrating my shadow side. I have got back in touch with cleaning my home even if it doesn't look much better and I feel much more energetic. So:

- When you're next feeling low, clean out a drawer, cupboard or shelf.
- Forego your dishwasher occasionally and remember what it's like to wash up.
- Go for a 'golden 10' – 10 minutes a day devoted to doing one task or more to keeping your house clean and fresh: hoovering, sweeping, polishing surfaces, throwing out old papers, dusting or taking one room and giving it a pretty good clean.

And if you do have good fortune, remember your shadow side. Celebrate the dark side of success by doing one dirty job. It really does keep you balanced.

'More and more of us earn our livelihood via our heads. We sit slumped all day in chairs, staring at computer screens or battling with machinery. Cleaning, which done properly is hard physical graft, provides a good healthy balance.'

JANE ALEXANDER, alternative health guru and author of *Spirit of the Home*

Defining idea...

How did it go?

Q   What is our 'dark side'?

A   It is simply the part of our personalities we don't show to the world. Mainly because rage, resentment and bitterness don't tend to make you the most popular girl at the party. When we only celebrate the positive side – our achievements – we are denying a huge part of ourselves. This is acted out in our homes: we expend all our energy on creating beautiful showpieces of homes, but increasingly ignoring the nuts and bolts of keeping them that way. Pretending that we don't have a bad side takes a lot of energy but it is the social norm. It's OK as long as we don't forget that the dark side is there. And the easiest way to remind ourselves of our, and everyone else's, dark side is to get grounded.

Q   My house is spotless and I do it all myself. So what should I do?

A   Nothing. If you feel that you are in touch with your shadow side. If not, try gardening. This idea is about physically grounding yourself in the everyday, and gardening fulfils that.

39

Big in Japan

Apparently, up to 10% of the Japanese population take the supplement Coenzyme Q10, but is curing tiredness really as easy as popping a pill?

Vitamin and mineral supplementation won't help if you're ignoring the basics of energy production. But they can be enough to fine-tune your vitality levels.

OPTION 1: COENZYME Q10

***Try this if ...* you eat well but you seem to have less energy as you get older**

Coenzyme Q10 is needed to produce energy in every cell and it's especially abundant in hard-working cells such as heart muscle. (When it was first discovered, scientists called it 'ubiquinone' because it was ubiquitous in nature.) It is found in all living creatures and concentrated in many foods. It's a catalyst in the complex chemical reactions that turn food into energy. It works with enzymes (hence 'coenzyme') to fire up chemical reactions that provide energy. It's so important that some doctors have mooted that it should be called vitamin Q.

Here's an idea for you... **Taking a multivitamin and mineral formulation should boost energy levels, especially during times when it's hard to eat well. A multi should usually be taken with food, ideally with breakfast, to ensure maximum absorption. Minerals in the form of carbonates and oxides tend to be less well absorbed. Look for formulations that include these in the form of ascorbates, citrates and gluconates, preferably.**

It also helps to neutralise the free radicals that are released during oxidation and damage cells – thus it is a powerful antioxidant. Quite extravagant claims are made for it – that it's anti-cancerous, works as an immune booster and can even stave off ageing – but it's mainly used as an energy booster and to treat heart conditions. Many doctors believe it should be prescribed alongside drugs such as statins for circulatory conditions as it helps them work effectively. A major study in Italy of heart-failure patients also found that it helped patients to sleep better after 90 days, although this could be related to alleviating heart failure symptoms.

Coenzyme Q10 is in our foods. It's especially rich in nuts and oils, but it is easily destroyed by cooking and storage. Having enough of it is also compounded by the fact that at about the age of 40, we find it harder to manufacture it. This could be one of the reasons our stamina tails off as we age.

Worth a try? You need to take Coenzyme Q10 for at least eight weeks before you'll feel the benefits. It should be taken with food as it's fat-soluble and this will aid absorption. A dose of around 50mcg twice a day is usual, although follow the instructions on the packet. It hasn't been extensively studied in pregnant and breast-feeding women so they should avoid it.

OPTION 2: AN ENERGY PRESCRIPTION

Try this if ... you've not been eating well and/or you are extremely tired. It combines some of the vitamins and minerals that are suspected to be involved in energy deficiency.

B-vitamin complex

The B vitamins are easily available in food, but even a small deficiency can cause a dip in energy and often goes undetected according to nutritionists. *Dose: take a B-vitamin complex twice a day with food.*

Vitamin C

This is a powerful energiser and also helps when you are depleted by periods of stress, alcohol or smoking. It supports the adrenal glands. *Dose: 500mg twice a day (can cause diarrhoea, cut down if too much).*

Magnesium

This is another oft-overlooked cause of lethargy. *Dose: 400mg a day (can cause diarrhoea, withdraw if too much).* Magnesium citrate is the most easily absorbed form. (Take a calcium supplement at the same time. Calcium and magnesium need to be balanced in the body for best results.)

Read more about ginseng in IDEA 22, *Herbal helpers*. Take it alongside vitamins mentioned here.

Try another idea...

'Three hundred years after the scientific revolution, the placebo is still the strongest force in medicine and, for the majority of patients, the major determinant in the outcome of healthcare.'
LEO GALLAND, renowned physician

Defining idea...

177

Q   Is there anything else I can try?

A   *Fish oils are the new wonder supplements, implicated in just about everything from increasing IQ to beating depression. They also help stamina
and boost the immune system. Try two teaspoons of cod liver oil a day, or
capsules as recommended. Vegetarians can take flaxseed oil from health
food shops.*

**Q   Is it true that chromium will boost my energy as well as burn off
fat?**

A   *Chromium's main claim to fame is that it helps balance blood-sugar levels
by boosting the effects of insulin, the hormone that transfers blood sugar
to the cells where it is burned. If you regularly get irritable and tired, especially when you don't eat, you could benefit from chromium, as it's useful
for those with low blood sugar. As for the weight loss, the jury's still out.
Those with diabetes should speak to their doctors before taking it. There
have been a few question marks over chromium's safety so before supple-
menting, you could experiment with getting more chromium from wholegrain cereals, potatoes, prunes, peanut butter, nuts, seafood and brewer's
yeast.*

40

Revamp your 'to do' list

**'To do' lists are essential for most of us but they can be
a huge drain on energy.**

The list that never seems to get any
shorter is not so much an aide-memoire
as a horrible reminder that we're running
fast but getting nowhere.

And what could be more dispiriting than that?

The other side, of course, is that 'to do' lists are incredibly useful tools for moti-
vating us and making us more productive. Having a clear plan for the day ahead
focuses the mind and puts you in control like nothing else. Whether you're a CEO,
freelance, stay-at-home parent or student, the well run 'to do' list will give you a
sense of full-capacity living.

But for it to work, you have to have a definite system. Try this one. It is based on the
advice given to 1930s magnate Charles Schwabb by a young man he challenged to
double his productivity. The young man told him to write down the six most crucial

Here's an idea for you...

Switch off your mobile for as long as you can comfortably get away with, but aim for at least an hour in the morning and an hour in the afternoon. These should be your high productivity times when you aim to really motor through your tasks. The act of switching of your mobile sends an unconscious message to your brain that this is time when your interests are the priority, and it helps to focus your mind on the task at hand.

tasks for each day in order of importance and work down the list. Then teach his staff to do the same. After a few weeks, the story goes that Schwabb sent a cheque for £25,000 to he young man, which was a huge sum then.

This idea works on the principle that we put off important stuff (or we work to others' agenda so we don't get round to what's important for us) and keep ourselves busy with lesser tasks to distract ourselves. But if we don't do the one important thing, no matter what we achieve, we'll feel dissatisfied at the end of the day. Instead of an abstract list of things to do that you attack randomly, switch the angle from what you *must* do to *when* you are going to do it.

HOW TO REVAMP YOUR 'TO DO' LIST

In your diary or a separate notebook, draw a line down the left hand side of the page to form a column and mark in the working hours of the day. This can be precise (9.30 to 10.30, 10.30 to 11.30) or loose (morning, afternoon). Now you're set to go.

- At the end of your working day, brew a cuppa, sit for a second, take a deep breath and gather your thoughts. Pat yourself on the back for what you have achieved today. Now. Swing your mind forward into tomorrow.

See IDEA 25, *Dealing with interruptions*, for more ideas on maximising your time.

Try another idea...

- Ask yourself what regular scheduled tasks or meetings you have for tomorrow. Block them off on your diary page.
- Remember to add in travelling time, lunch and relaxation.
- What is your major task? What *must* you do tomorrow? That gets priority and should be done first thing if possible. Set aside a realistic block of time (err on the side of caution). Be precise.
- Put in specific times for phone calls/e-mails. It is more time effective to do these in two or three blocks rather than breaking concentration and doing it ad hoc during the day.
- What's your next most important task? Is there room in your day? If you have time left, you can schedule in other tasks, but be realistic.
- For each week have a short list of brief one-off tasks (phone calls, paying bills, birthday cards) and if you have a few down minutes, slot them in.

'Energy and persistence alter all things.'

BENJAMIN FRANKLIN

Defining idea...

Q **I just have too much to do. How can I focus on what's most important?**

A *It sounds like stress has got to you. This idea is good for this because it makes you focus on exactly how much time you've got. A fatal mistake of the stress-laden and those of perfectionist tendency is to think time is elastic – that it will stretch to fit what you have to do. Now make the priority your time off during the day: lunchtime and fifteen minutes each morning and afternoon are essential. Forcing yourself to stop and do an activity that you enjoy will seem a hopeless waste of time, but it will, if you persevere, help you get perspective. This is one of those classic situations where you don't have to believe this advice for it to work; you just have to do it.*

Q **Schwabb got to do six tasks. Why do you just talk about one, maybe two?**

A *Because I find it energising. It's a mind trick. It gives me energy to see each day in terms of one task that I have to complete. As I write this, it is 9.23 a.m. and the one thing I told myself to do today was complete writing this idea. So I've achieved my one priority already. Of course, I'll carry on and do more. But because I've already achieved my one priority, I feel like a winner and I'm full of energy for this project. By keeping a realistic goal in mind – a very realistic goal – I get a kick. If I set my goals too high, I'd fail and I'd feel overwhelmed by all I had to do.*

41

Colour your life energetic

According to Ayurvedic medicine, our energy levels depend on our *chakras* – energy channels – being open.

Each chakra is linked to a colour and using that colour as a meditation tool opens the chakra.

Whatever you make of that, colour is a powerful aid to visualisation, and using colour in this way can impact positively on your energy in a matter of minutes.

WHEN YOU FEEL FRAGMENTED AND NEED ENERGY TO OVERCOME FEELINGS OF BEING OVERWHELMED

Red is associated with the root *chakra*. Red helps your sense of security and your motivation to get things done. Sit quietly for a few moments, with your feet firmly on the floor, breathe deeply. Imagine each breath as being deep, crimson red, suffusing your body, filling and gathering in your belly, and then travelling further down. See the breath going right down to your feet.

WHEN YOU NEED AN INSTANT ENERGY BOOST

Orange is associated with the sacral *chakra* and is linked to your sexual energy and optimism. It's also the colour therapists most often claim will give you energy. Try a touch of orange in your wardrobe: a scarf, handbag or pair of gloves. Or follow the trick adopted in Scandinavian countries of having a huge bowl of tangerines on your desk: the colour and the scent both energise. Or have a vase of orange tulips where you can see them easily.

WHEN YOU FEEL 'STUCK' BUT NEED THE ENERGY TO GET ON

Yellow is associated with the solar plexus. Focussing on it will help you deal with unresolved feelings, and with letting go of issues that might be blocking your energy. Take a lemon-scented bath, and lie back in it taking deep 'belly' breaths. Imagine you are breathing in sunshine with each breath. As you breathe out, imagine resentments, bitterness and regret floating away.

WHEN A RELATIONSHIP IS DRAINING YOUR ENERGY

Green is associated with the heart *chakra*. An open heart *chakra* encourages self-acceptance and allows relationships to flow easily. Go to the country for the day or to the park for a walk at lunchtime. Or lie under a tree and lose yourself in the green canopy above you. Mixing yourself a 'green' juice – using green vegetables – is good for your body and spirit.

Here's an idea for you... Have bowls of pink, purple and white (or cream) flowers around your home, or on your desk. This combination is believed by colour therapists to raise a calm, focused energy that helps you relax while getting things done.

WHEN YOU WANT TO COMMUNICATE IDEAS WITH ENERGY AND FORCE

Blue is associated with the throat *chakra*. It allows easy communication and an increase in creativity. If you have ideas that you want to bring to fruition, buy some large sheets of pale blue paper and arm yourself with blue crayons, pencils, pens and paints. Brainstorm ideas. Draw them if that's easier than writing. You can use the power of blue to talk to yourself when you feel 'stuck' in your life. Draw or write – again in blue – how your life would be in an ideal universe, in one, five and ten years from now.

Combine these colour meditations with those in IDEA 5, *Stand tall, breathe deep*, for a double whammy effect.

Try another idea...

WHEN A DIFFICULT DECISION IS SAPPING YOUR ENERGY AND BREAKING YOUR CONCENTRATION

Purple is the 'third eye' *chakra*, associated with intuition. When it is open and energy is flowing easily through it, you know instinctively what direction to take. Wearing shades of purple – lavender and violet – subconsciously makes you more in touch with your gut feelings. When you are faced with a dilemma, try lighting a purple candle and throwing a dice or coin to help you clarify your thoughts. Pose questions, allowing the coin or dice to determine 'yes' or 'no'. The point is not to hand your direction over to chance, but to listen to the reactions you have to the throw of the dice: your initial responses will help you decide what you really want to do.

WHEN YOU NEED TO RESTORE ENERGY LEVELS AND CRAVE PEACE OF MIND

White is associated with the crown *chakra*. It is associated with spirituality; when it is open, you feel tranquil. Use white and off-white to decorate one room of your home where you can go to feel clear and peaceful. Or simply imagine yourself bathed in white light, healing and dissolving troubles and worries.

'I cannot pretend to feel impartial about colours. I rejoice with the brilliant ones and am genuinely sorry for the poor browns.'
WINSTON CHURCHILL

Defining idea...

185

How did it go?

Q   Is there any evidence for all of this?

A   Common sense will tell you that different colours have an effect on your mood – imagine living in a black room for weeks on end. Some studies that I think are quite interesting focus on the placebo response evoked by different colours of pills given to patients. Some, but not all, studies have shown that if orange, red or yellow pills are given to people, they feel energetic in a dynamic, go-getting way; give them blue, green or purple, and there is a tranquillising and restful effect. The association in our mind with these colours goes deep.

Q   Instead of doing the meditations, can I simply dress in the appropriate colours?

A   Yes, and be aware that the colours you reach for when you're dressing may be a clue to what you think your energy needs are going to be later on that day. Red – you may be feeling a bit below par and need a boost; blue – you know you need focus and concentration; green – you feel fairly relaxed; yellow – your self-esteem may need a boost, and you are wearing this bright colour to disguise it; purple – you want to conserve your energy and be left alone. However, whatever colour you choose to wear, make sure that the hue of the colour suits you. Most of us can wear most colours, but only certain shades of the colour. Wear one that suits you, not one that 'wears' you. It's, literally, wearing.

42

Supermarket savvy

Turn your supermarket shop into an energy-boosting adventure.

Live a little — eat more! Choosing from a wide variety of foods will boost your energy. (And changing your variety of crisp doesn't count.)

The average person eats only around twenty different foods. How dull is that? Nutritionists say we should eat from the widest variety of foods possible because, unsurprisingly, that will result in getting the optimal number of nutrients. You should be looking to make your choice from between 60 to 70 different foods on a regular basis!

There are two advantages when it comes to your energy levels in mixing it up.

1   You will be eating a cornucopia of energy-boosting nutrients.
2   You will render your shopping trips a lot more interesting.

The nutrients that are vital for energy are the B vitamins, vitamin C, magnesium, iron and chromium. Shopping with the following lists in mind will ensure you're topped up with all of them.

THE TOP 10 MULTI-TASKERS

To make it really easy when you're shopping *add three of these a week* to your shopping trolley and mix it up: select another three next week. They have been chosen to supply a good mix of B vitamins, magnesium, iron and chromium – the nutrients especially crucial for energy release.

- Bran flakes – packed with iron, B vitamins and vitamin C.
- Beef – iron, chromium. (Liver is another good food for supplying the energy nutrients.)
- Wholegrain rice and bread – B vitamins and magnesium.
- Chick peas – magnesium and iron.
- Oats – vitamin B and magnesium.
- Sardines – magnesium and iron.
- Quorn – loaded with one of the key B vitamins.
- Turkey – vitamin B12 and iron.
- Nuts and seeds – mix and match different types for 'broad spectrum' cover. Pumpkin seeds are a particularly good source of iron.
- Rye bread – good for iron and B vitamins.

Here's an idea for you...

Stick to the perimeter of your supermarket like glue. Almost always, the 'real' food is focused on the outside of the store, the junk in the middle aisles. Leave your trolley at the end of the aisle when you go to buy cleaning fluids and pet food. Having to carry junk food back to your trolley makes it less likely that you'll pick them up in the first place as it's a lot harder than just tossing them in.

TWELVE CRACKING VITAMIN C SOURCES

Choose three a week, on top of your usual foodstuffs. Mix them up. These all supply more than 20mg per 100g of food: blackcurrants, bran flakes, Brussels sprouts, cabbage (raw has double), cauliflower, citrus fruits, kiwi fruit, mango, raw red and orange peppers, raspberries, strawberries and watercress.

SIX TOP SNACKS

These combine the all-important energy combo: protein with carbohydrate. Stock up with enough of these so that when you need a between-meal pick-up, you can reach for a snack that will fill you up without sending your blood sugar soaring (which leads to a slump in energy later). Some of these are a bit odd at first, but just try eating one of these snacks mid-morning and mid-afternoon, and you'll be amazed at how satisfying they are.

- Two oatcakes with peanut butter
- Nuts – a good handful maybe with a few raisins or sultanas
- A stick of celery spread with cream or cottage cheese
- Slices of apple spread thinly with peanut or other nut butter
- A vegetable juice with a few nuts on the side
- A boiled egg and a couple of rye crispbreads or a slice of rye bread.

OTHER GREAT ENERGY FOODS TO ADD TO YOUR SHOPPING LIST ON A REGULAR BASIS

Eggs (protein/vitamin B); pumpkin seeds (a great source of zinc); mackerel (best source of omega-3, which is the wonder nutrient of the moment, and also a great source of protein); bulgur (a good source of slow-releasing carbohydrate for long-lasting energy); Marmite (good for B vitamins); basil (beloved by herbalists for its uplifting qualities); artichoke (rich in vitamin C and magnesium); beetroot (high in vitamin C, magnesium, iron and B vitamins); kale (packed with iron and B vitamins); lentils (loaded with magnesium); celery (has special phytochemicals that are good for energy and improving mood).

Between 1 and 4% of people in the UK are anaemic. Turn to IDEA 48, *Tired ... or ill?*, for more on getting enough iron.

Try another idea…

'There is no love sincerer than the love of food.'
GEORGE BERNARD SHAW

Defining idea…

189

How did it go?

Q   You seem very keen on bran flakes. Why?

A   *I'm even keener on All-Bran, because it has nearly all the nutrients of bran flakes but a lower GI (between 21–30). Low GI foods cause minimum disruption of your blood sugar levels, minimising your chances of a sugar crash mid-afternoon. Porridge is good for this too (GI is around 31–40) – the real McCoy that needs cooking rather than instant, but it still only takes a couple of minutes so it's as near to a fast food as you can get. Shredded wheat has less salt and a GI of over 70, around that of bran flakes. All other cereals should be considered as treats.*

Q   I don't know how to cook half the vegetables. What can I do?

A   *What worked for me was writing a column that included monthly recommendations of what was seasonal. It meant I had to cook at least one new recipe every month. Even this brings a sense of adventure to your shopping. These are some seasonal foods in the UK.*

- *January: turnips, scallops, parsnips*
- *February: chicory, celeriac, cabbage*
- *March: rhubarb, radishes, purple sprouting broccoli*
- *April: lamb, rosemary, spinach*
- *May: asparagus, broad beans, cherries*
- *June: strawberries, gooseberries, courgettes*
- *July: blueberries, fennel, aubergines*
- *August: greengages, basil, peppers*
- *September: damsons, plums, autumn lamb*
- *October: figs, elderberries, watercress*
- *November: chestnuts, beetroot, cranberries*
- *December: pomegranates, red cabbage, celery*

43

Just a minute ...

One-minute bursts of energy, cunningly slipped into your usual routine, will revolutionise your energy levels.

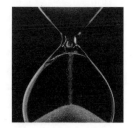

And if you combine these with the latest research on 'activity' rather than exercise, you'll get fit too, without even trying ...

Just about the fastest way of feeling instantly more energetic is to get the blood pounding in your ears and the breath whizzing in and out of your lungs. A quick burst of activity is also great for dissipating stress hormones. Learning how to navigate through your day, building in little pockets of activity is one of the surest ways of becoming more stress-resilient and better prepared to cope with the demands of your life.

This idea offers a blueprint of how to slot one-minute bursts of activity and slightly longer sessions throughout your day. Your energy levels will soar, but there's an added bonus. You can also feel smug that you're looking after your body as well as those who exercise. Research from an exercise research centre in Dallas shows that those who are active for 30 minutes three times a week are as healthy as those who exercise at a gym for 30 minutes three times a week. This idea has been accepted by our own Health Education Authority, and they recommend being active for 20–30 minutes every day as being a reasonable goal for staying healthy. Activity

Here's an idea for you...

Here's a physical and a mental energiser. March on the spot for one minute. According to self-esteem expert Gael Lindenfield, marching on the spot for one minute not only gets your heart beating fast, it has mental benefits too. The left–right action stimulates the connections between your brain's hemispheres and speeds up your thinking.

means gardening, walking briskly to work, climbing stairs rather than using lifts, playing football with the kids, stretching to dust on a high shelf. The easiest way to do this, I find, is to build in some 10-minute-or-so activity sessions and, every hour or so, do a minute's exercise for its energy-boosting effects.

If you want more energy. Cast your eye over the following programme and look for one-minute boosters. Try these or something similar and feel the difference in your energy levels.

If you want to get fit too. You do need a plan. You need to know that you're doing your 30 minutes or else you end up climbing one flight of stairs and kidding yourself it's enough. Here is a sample timetable of how you could build in enough activity.

RE-ENERGISE YOUR DAY

- *7 a.m. – One-minute booster.* Here's a trick. Place your alarm clock at the bottom of the bed. Stretch to reach it. Now you've started, don't stop. Spend a minute stretching in bed. Children stretch when they wake up. So do animals. Movement stimulates the waking part of the brain and makes getting up easier.
- *7.15 a.m. – Ten minutes 'being active'.* Do some yoga stretches such as the sun salutation or some resistance training with some light weights. Increasing blood flow

and raising your body temperature will help wake you up.

■ *8 a.m. – One-minute booster.* While you're waiting for the kettle to boil, do star jumps for one minute.

■ *9 a.m. – Ten minutes 'being active'.* Walk to a newsagent five minutes from your home or desk for your morning paper. There and back equals ten minutes' activity.

■ *11.30 a.m. – One-minute booster.* While sitting at your desk do some abdominal 'pull-ins'. Sit straight in your chair. Breathe in and pull your navel in and up, hold and let out. Each one should take a second. Aim for 60 in the morning (and fit in another 60 in the afternoon).

■ *1 p.m. – Lunch.* If you were going to be really good, you could fit in a quick walk, gym visit or run up and down the stairs a few times. But hey! You're doing so well, you can head straight for the pub.

■ *3 p.m. – One-minute booster.* Stretch out the tension in your shoulders by standing straight and clasping your hands behind your back.

■ *5 p.m. – One-minute booster.* Get a refreshing drink, say, a green tea. While you're waiting for the kettle, run up and down stairs for one minute.

■ *6 p.m. – Ten minutes 'being active'.* If you're going to exercise properly this is a good time to do it. If not, do some activity when you get home – gardening or running up and down stairs.

Congratulations. Not only are you more energetic – you're an exerciser, too!

Turn to IDEA 24, *Good morning, sunshine,* for the salutation to the sun routine. It's a perfect five-minute start to the day.

Try another idea...

'The best effect of any book is that it excites the reader to self-activity.'
THOMAS CARLYLE

Defining idea...

How did it go? **Q** **I can follow your ideas for later in the day. What can help me do it in the morning?**

A *Blood rushing to the head really works to wake you up which is why the Salutation to the Sun is such a winner. But if you can't do that, try this. Lie back and raise your legs up against the wall for support. Shoot along until your buttocks rest against the wall. Stay there for a minute, breathing deeply. This is energising and relaxing. And if your bed is next to a wall, you don't even have to get out of bed.*

Q **There aren't any stairs in my office. Any idea what I can do to energise myself at work mid-afternoon?**

A *Nip to the loo and do sixty star jumps. Yes, you will look a fool if your boss catches you, but live dangerously. She might have already left for the day and the boost to your circulation will energise you for the journey home. I have escaped to the loo at work and done the legs-up-against-the-wall described in the answer above when I'm having a bad day, and I've always found it to work. That could get some even funnier looks from your boss. But in my experience, there is always somewhere you can escape to for a minute, if you're inventive enough.*

44

Every breath you take ...

... is another opportunity to energise yourself.

(If you know something about the power of scent.)

Your sense of smell is rooted in one of the very oldest parts of the brain from an evolutionary point of view. The limbic area is connected with memory, emotion and sleep. And, with a little know-how, all of these centres can be 'triggered' in order to boost your energy. Scent is inhaled via millions of sensitive cells that line the nasal passages and these send messages straight to the brain. Which means that the response is near instantaneous.

Scent will work for you without any conscious thought of your own which is why it's such a useful energising tool. In spring, a bowl of strongly scented hyacinth on your desk will help you get through a difficult day more smoothly. In summer, lying on a newly mown grass for ten minutes will energise you faster than a coffee. In autumn, burning apple logs rather than coal will lift your spirits if you're lucky enough to have an open fire; and in winter, use pine scented candles to evoke the very spirit of Christmas. All of these scents will energise you even if they weren't part of your childhood. The power of smell to make us feel better is one of the best arguments for collective consciousness – the idea that we are all linked by common ancestral memories.

Here's an idea for you...

When you're tired, you often feel cold and tense. Warm herbs counteract this. Drop two tablespoons of powdered ginger under the hot tap when you're having a bath. It is an energising hot bath to boost circulation and relax muscles while pepping you up. It may make skin flush but the water needs to be hot or the ginger doesn't dissolve.

You can take it one more step by buying a few aromatherapy oils for everyday use. Smell is such a powerful sense that if you associate a certain aroma with a particular emotion, then every time you smell that smell, you'll feel the same emotion. You can use this to your advantage. One of the best pieces of advice I was given was by the noted aromatherapist Robert Tisserand. His advice was to take lavender aromatherapy oil on holiday and use it every day, a few drops in lotion or on sunburn (lavender is one of the few oils you can use directly on skin). Then whenever I smelled lavender when I got back home, I would immediately be taken back mentally to my holiday and feel the associated feelings of relaxation and general brilliance. It worked, and I have adapted this idea to 'hardwire' my brain for energetic thoughts by connecting the scent of the oil *may chang* to times when I feel particularly energised and happy. If the sun's shining and I'm out for a walk, if I'm effortlessly achieving all my tasks, when I feel in the 'flow' with energy to spare, I have a sniff of *may chang* or burn it in a diffuser in my home. Whenever I smell *may chang*, I feel energised and so on days like this when I'm feeling a bit flat, it automatically works to make things easier. Select a scent that you like and hardwire your brain in the same way.

Note to men: this idea isn't just for the 'ladeez'. You'll be pleased to hear that the scents that supply energy are for the most part unisex – some are staples of the male aftershave industry because of their clean, invigorating scents.

TO RAISE PHYSICAL ENERGY

When you're feeling tired and sluggish, fresh and spicy aromas will boost you. Add two drops of the following to a tablespoon of almond oil and rub into your body.

- *Black pepper.* Black pepper is traditionally used as a muscle rub before and after exercise.
- *Ginger.* When we're cold, we tense up which is draining. Ginger stimulates circulation and warms you up.

TO RAISE MENTAL ENERGY

'Woody' scents such as pine, cypress and eucalyptus are great for concentration.

- *Rosemary.* Particularly brilliant for mental clarity.
- *Peppermint.* Add a few drops to a base oil, carry it with you and rub it on your temples when you're under stress. It helps if you're prone to tension headaches as it opens the sinuses and relieves pressure.

TO RAISE SPIRITUAL ENERGY

All citrus scents are wonderful for lifting your mood and taking you to a new high.

- Lemon sharpens your mind.
- Lime is good for when you're feeling flat because of stress and feeling 'nervy'.

Combine aromatherapy with the colour meditation in IDEA 41, *Colour your life energetic.*

Try another idea…

'Smell is a potent wizard that transports you across thousands of miles and all the years you have lived.'

HELEN KELLER

Defining idea…

197

**Q   I've tried adding a few drops of pine to my bath but it isn't work-
ing. I'm still exhausted. What can I do?**

A   *When you're low, use clary sage (but not if you're pregnant or breast feeding) and geranium. These are both very good for lifting mood especially
when you're exhausted. Geranium especially is know to restore balance
when you're particularly up against it.*

**Q   I can't be doing with all this fiddling around with oils. Any other
suggestions?**

A   *It really doesn't have to be a drag. Try this for a week and see if it doesn't
convert you. Try a cup of Earl Grey tea as a pick up mid-afternoon. Add a
slice of lemon (if it's not too much of a fiddle!). Early Grey gets its distinctive scent from bergamot which is great for energy and keeping you
focused. The lemon gives you a lift, too. This little scent ritual is very helpful in a stressful day. You might be moved to buy a few drops of peppermint or pine essential oil. Sprinkle on a hanky each morning and when you
feel unfocused and tired, take a sniff. Add a couple of drops of oil to your
normal body lotion or moisturiser. And I honestly can't see how it's a fiddle
to add a few drops to a bath. Think of aromatherapy as an everyday, easy
tool – not a special 'spa-night' treat.*

45

Go for the glow

Short cuts to re-energising your skin.

Anything that gives you a healthy boost in energy should also do miracles for your looks. But if your skin isn't glowing as much as you'd like, then try this.

The basics of building more energy are also those necessary for looking your best; adequate sleep, plenty of good quality food especially fruit and vegetables, and some regular exercise to boost your circulation (increased blood flow to your cheeks helps enormously). Once they're in place, what else can you do?

Luminous skin depends on how much light your skin absorbs in relation to how much it reflects. For it to reflect well, there has to be a good scaffolding of collagen fibres that allows your skin to 'mirror' light back. Unfortunately, collagen begins to break down after the age of about 35 to 40. It breaks down even faster in those that smoke and those that overdo UV sun exposure and these should be the first bad habits you eliminate if you are serious about supercharging your skin's appearance.

This three step plan should help improve your skin in a matter of days.

POLISH YOUR SKIN

Dead skin cells make your skin dull because they don't reflect light. Smooth them away with a religiously-adhered to cleansing programme – known as exfoliation. Scrubs can be too harsh especially for older skins and the best way is to remove them gently every night with your normal cleanser. Try cleansers that contain alpha- or beta-hydroxy acids that lift away dead skin cells. An alternative is a thick cleanser which you massage in and then remove with a flannel, exfoliating as you go. The extremely expensive Eve Lom cleanser is the original and my favourite. I am too ashamed to tell people how much it costs and I use supermarket moisturizers and make-up so that I can justify its expense (but a pot does last me six months). There are cheaper versions available – try any where a flannel is part of the package. Liz Earle's (available on the internet) is also good.

Here's an idea for you... **Eyedrops that get rid of blood shot eyes are your quickest route to a re-energised look. Navy eyeliner is the second quickest. It neutralises 'red eye syndrome' better than black or brown and makes the whites of the eyes zing. On the whole keep makeup to the upper lids and lashes. The eyes of people looking at you will be dragged upwards, away from sagging.**

EVEN OUT SKIN TONE

One of the reasons skin doesn't reflect light is the increase in pigmentation (melanin) as you get older due to cumulative sun damage. The most obvious suggestion is to wear a moisturizer with sun protection all year round, and on bright days, sun lotion on your face every time you go out in the sun. A hat is even better.

Glucosamine (the same supplement that is used for arthritis) is being touted as a new treatment for dull skin, delivering results in around eight weeks. You can find it in lotions now (Olay do one). Another nutrient known to minimise ageing pigmentation is niacinamide (Vitamin B3).

Your skin won't glow without sleep. See IDEA 6, *How to get enough sleep.*

Try another idea…

REBUILD YOUR SCAFFOLDING

Collagen damage can be repaired with retinoids – a form of vitamin A. There are many lotions available that contain retinoids, generally the more expensive they are the more active ingredients they contain. Retinoids don't go well with sunlight so it's best to use them at night. Which is a good idea anyway because skin cell regeneration is slightly higher at night: that makes it the perfect time to apply treatment creams.

That's the basic skin care routine but it's not just dull skin that makes us look tired. Sagging, lifeless skin is for many of us more ageing than wrinkles. One solution? Ditch your pillow. Squashing your face at night eventually leads to permanent lines. A small study of Japanese women discovered that we have more wrinkles in the afternoon than the morning, and the scientists therefore assumed that gravity plays a powerful role in causing wrinkles. Ergo: lying flat on your back, preferably without a pillow, will combat the effects of gravity that were at work during the day. I have tried this because I suffer from droopy eyes – and it worked. Another idea is to keep eye cream in the fridge and one of those gel-packs to wear over the eyes in the bath. Coldness combats under-eye puffiness.

'Beauty is in the eye of the beholder and it may be necessary from time to time to give a stupid or misinformed beholder a black eye.'

MISS PIGGY

Defining idea…

How did it go?

Q   Tried all that. Why doesn't it make much difference?

A   *Time to hit your local beauty salon. Microdermabrasion and glycolic peels polish the skin and even out skin tone. If you're really serious, deep lines and furrows due to collagen breakdown can be helped by fillers such as Botox and Restylane that last between three and six months. Some recent research even showed that Restylane may stimulate collagen production so the results may be longer-lasting than first thought! However, I would stick to a good routine for a while before embarking on more costly measures. Very few people who do – and watch their health in general – have bad skin.*

Q   What if I can't afford much in the way of beauty products?

A   *The best one-minute facelift is a good plucking of the eye brow shape into a natural arch. By exposing more of the brow bone, you 'open' up the eyes. But don't go crazy or you'll look weird. Many beauty salons offer a brow re-shape inexpensively. Once you've got the shape you can carry on the good work at home. If even that's beyond your purse, put foundation over your natural brows and draw in with water-soluble felt pen different shapes of brow until you find one that suits you. (This is one to do in private.) Then carefully pluck the hairs that are 'under' the line. Never pluck above the line. NB. Using soft brown shadow and a little brush to carefully 'feather' in brows will give a far more natural effect than pencil.*

46

Where do you go for energy?

When we need to lift our energy we do one of two things – we go inwards or we go outwards.

Understanding how we operate means there's always a place where we can go when we need an energy boost.

This quiz will help you decide where you 'go'.

1. When you've been working steadily on a project for a couple of hours, would you prefer to:
   (a) take a break and chat with a colleague or friend?
   (b) listen to some music or sit quietly with a cuppa mulling over what you've done and what you want to do next?
2. When you are stuck on an idea, do you find that it's:
   (a) nearly always useful to bounce ideas off someone else?
   (b) rarely useful to talk to anyone – you think best alone?
3. If you have to stay home to work for a couple of days, do you:
   (a) feel you're missing out?
   (b) feel delighted, to get the chance to work uninterrupted?

4   When you meet new people do you:
   (a) talk as much as you listen?
   (b) listen more than you talk?
5   When you're having a good time, do you:
   (a) want to keep going until other people begin to fade?
   (b) enjoy yourself up to a point but get tired and after a while feel you need
       some space?
6   Do you usually:
   (a) talk freely without planning what you're going to say?
   (b) think what point you want to make before opening your mouth?

It won't come as much of a surprise to discover that those who mainly answered
(a)s are extroverts and those (b)s are introverts. Psychologists believe that you are
one or the other, but that there is a scale: you may have a mixture of (a)s and (b)s
but you will probably be able to identify
where your real preference lies. The big clue is
that, when it comes to restoring energy levels,
extroverts and introverts differ in one fundamental respect: extroverts will do so best
by reaching out to other people; introverts
need time and space alone to sort through
their thoughts and feelings. Problems arise
when you don't realise your *modus operandi*.
You aren't working with their personality, but
against it.

Here's an idea for you...

**Take your understanding into
your work and you'll find life
will flow more easily. Would
your introvert colleague
prefer it if you emailed her
an idea, rather than burst
into her office to tell her?
Would your extrovert boss
prefer a presentation to key
staff rather than a carefully
written report? You may find
it more difficult in the short
term, but working around
other people's preferences
may save you energy in the
long run.**

EXTROVERTS: 'THE PEOPLE WHO NEED PEOPLE'

Learn more about psychology typing in IDEA 30, *What kind of time traveller are you?*

Try another idea...

If you are an extrovert, you get your energy from the world around you. You get energy by directing your attention outwards, looking for affirmation and a platform. You don't really feel that you've had a good idea unless someone else agrees with you; you must give other people the opportunity to react to your work or you find it hard to get excited by it. Your personality expands and you 'become more yourself' when you have an arena in which to assert yourself. You feed off other people's energy and ideas

Watch out: You may be perfectly capable of spending time alone but it will drain you. For example, become too involved in a work project so that you cut out friends, and you won't get more work done: you'll grind to a halt. If you have an introvert partner, remember that your need for company is as important as their need to be alone. If they don't want to socialise or go out much, you may have to go alone or you'll get mightily frustrated.

INTROVERTS: 'I WANT TO BE ALONE'

If you are an introvert, you get your energy from focussing on your inner world of ideas and experiences. Reflecting on your thoughts, memories, feelings and ideas gives you more energy. Other people's opinions are not as important to you as what you think and feel yourself. While extroverts are energised by taking action, you are energised by contemplation.

'Jung observed that individuals tend to focus their energy and be energised more by the external world of people, experience and activity or more by the internal world of ideas, memories and emotions.'
ISABEL BRIGGS MYERS, psychologist

Defining idea...

205

Watch out: Introverts are so involved in their inner world that they don't realise the effect they have on other people. You are the 'strong, silent' types, the 'difficult, complex' people. Your withdrawal into yourself can be particularly hard for the extroverts in your life, and you may spend a lot of energy placating them when just a little attention when they wanted it would have averted a major misunderstanding.

How did it go?

Q   I'm still not sure where I fall. Any clues?

A   If you went to a party and saw someone you were attracted to, would you immediately start plotting to talk to them, or would you be slightly dreading having to talk to them because you like the look of them so much? I attended a workshop where we were asked this question. The differences were marked. Even very shy extroverts felt that at some point they would talk to the object of their desire. Even confident introverts believed that they'd have avoided them all night unless someone else had intervened.

Q   I answered equally introvert and extrovert. Can you be both?

A   Psychologists would say no. Some introverts love to party and don't understand why they become bad-tempered and exhausted while others are raring to go. Some extroverts love to spend time alone and wonder why, after a weekend they had set aside for rest, spent watching movies and reading, they feel horrible. All it would take to turn around their weekend is going to a cinema or arranging to meet a friend for a drink. Experiment when you're tired. Try reaching out and going inwards. Whatever energises you quicker is no doubt the best clue.

47

Be irresistible

The ability to draw others towards you effortlessly saves you the sweat of having to go to them. Result!

The secret to magnetism is dead simple — love yourself. And remember, high self-esteem isn't a constant; it's a work in progress.

Imagine if life just got easier. If the things you wanted in life seemed to flow towards you effortlessly. That's what the father of life coaching, US guru, Thomas Leonard, called 'irresistible attraction'. Which is a fabulous way of saying 'sky-high self-esteem'.

Without self-esteem you feel helpless, depressed, isolated. Life seems difficult and you don't feel other people care about you enough. Needless to say, it's a major bummer and brings your energy levels crashing down.

Fluctuating self-esteem is a major energy drainer without us realising it. We struggle on, feeling rubbish without really knowing why. Which is a shame, because

Here's an idea for you... **Set aside half an hour and write down every single thing you've been successful at or that you've completed successfully. Put anything on the list as long as it's meaningful to you. Finding a good dentist could be as much of a success as getting a promotion at work. When you run out of steam, look over the list and write down the qualities you needed to achieve each success – perseverance, courage, quick wit. Return to this list until you have at least 100 successes – and then give yourself a really nice reward for being so darn successful.**

making a few simple steps to feel better about ourselves can boost our energy immediately and that makes us more attractive to others. Life gets easier and we need to expend less energy to get through the day. Keeping a beady eye on our fluctuating self-esteem levels is a win-win situation energetically speaking.

Answer 'yes' or 'no' to these statements based on how you're feeling *now, today*– not how you felt last week, last year or last millennium.

1   Does life seem unnecessarily complicated?
2   Do all your attempts to make life better seem to get stuck?
3   Do you feel you're at the mercy of your family, job or other people?
4   Are you feeling slightly sick at the thought of all you have to achieve by the end of the week?
5   Do you feel that, if you want something, you can make it happen?
6   Do you feel that you are expressing who you really are through your image, home, work or interests?

Answer 'no' to the first four questions and 'yes' to questions 5 and 6, and you can skip this idea – for now. 'Yes' to the first four questions; 'no' to questions 5 or 6, and your self-esteem could use some work.

The good news is you can start right now. You'll have higher self-esteem by the time you go to bed tonight.

Look to IDEA 11, *Finding work to make your heart sing*, if your job is lowering your self-esteem.

Try another idea...

MAKE A DIFFERENCE – IT MAKES YOU GLORIOUSLY ATTRACTIVE

One characteristic of people with low self-esteem is that, deep down, they don't think it matters if they exist or not. Those with healthy self-esteem know they make a difference to the world. Easiest way of doing it? Pay a genuine compliment and then 'big' it up. Tell the bloke who makes your coffee how good it is, and let his manager overhear. Compliment your assistant on a job well done, then email your boss to let her know about his good work. Paying compliments makes you powerful. You remember the person who gave you a heartfelt compliment for the rest of your life. Don't you want to be that kind of memorable person?

DITCH THE MARTYRDOM – IT'S DEEPLY UNATTRACTIVE

All of us do things we don't want to do, but some of us get caught in a trap of working to other people's agendas too much of the time. And that's majorly exhausting. Think of one chore you really don't want to do: visit your aunt, help at the school fête, paint the bedroom. Now remember – it's optional. Pretty much everything in life is. Cancel it and do something that makes you happy instead. When 'duty' tasks mount up, we feel overwhelmed and out of control. Saying 'no' means you start to question every single time you say 'yes'. Saying 'no' to other people and 'yes' to yourself is very, very energising.

'The more you touch other people's lives, the more attractive you become.'
THOMAS LEONARD, coaching guru

Defining idea...

Q   **Surely your self-esteem doesn't pop up and down like a lift?**

A   *More of a wave than a lift. If I were to take the quiz above today – not tomorrow, not next week – then I'd give the wrong answer to three out of six questions. It's an energy drain but I might not realise it because I'm toddling along thinking 'my self esteem is high' – which it usually is. All it takes is one bad relationship, one bad boss or one bad blow-out in McDonald's to leave our self-esteem less than sparkling, and to feel rubbish for the whole of that day. This idea is about learning to monitor those days and take action to feel better asap.*

Q   **My self-esteem is low a lot. Is there anything more I can do?**

A   *Write down fifty words you would like to apply to yourself: joyful, optimistic, strong, intuitive, confident. Now take each word in turn, say out loud 'I am.' How true does that sound to you? If it's very, true score 2; moderately, score 1; not at all, score 0. Look at the 2s. Affirm those positive feelings. Look at the others. Imagine how you'd be if you had scored 2 on them. Now pick a couple and try to 'act as if'. This is incredibly powerful and the basis of the behavioural therapy NLP. Act like the person you want to be, copy their behaviour. One day you'll find you're not acting!*

48

Tired ... or ill?

Yes, you're tired. You're always tired. And now you're beginning to wonder if it could be a sign of something more sinister ...

How can you tell the difference between the sort of tiredness that means you've been overdoing it and the sort of tiredness that means you're ill?

ACTION PLAN

1   If persistent tiredness is accompanied by pain or unexplained weight loss, you should see your doctor as soon as possible for a check-up.
2   Go back to energy basics. The most common causes of exhaustion in young-ish adults is lack of good quality sleep, lack of space in your life, and lack of good food. If you're still tired after two weeks of TLC, see your doctor to explore further possibilities.

Here's an idea for you...
The two most overlooked causes of unexplained tiredness are reaction to medication (including alternative therapies) – and not realising you're pregnant. Discount both first.

WHAT KIND OF TIRED ARE YOU?

A gradual-onset tiredness that creeps up on you

Anything else? Needing to go to the loo more often, excessive thirst, weight loss, genital itching or thrush.

Could be? Diabetes.

Diabetes is the disease with a 'silent million' sufferers. A million have it; another million are undiagnosed. It's also a disease on the rise; sedentary lifestyles and an overdependence on processed food are contributing factors and more people than ever in their forties are discovering they've got it. If you are over forty, or you have other risk factors such as a family history or being overweight, your doctor should be happy to test you for diabetes if you suspect if it's at the root of your tiredness.

Lethargic and having difficulty concentrating

Anything else? Shortness of breath, dizziness.

Could be? Anaemia.

The tissues of your body need oxygen, which is carried to them by the red blood cells. Red blood cells need iron, so shortage of iron is one cause of anaemia. Menstruating women are most at risk, but anyone can get anaemia, especially if their diet isn't supplying enough iron. Eat more iron-rich food – red meat, fortified cereals and dried fruit – and take a multivitamin with iron in it. The medical line is that you have to have full-blown anaemia to suffer from chronic

Check out IDEA 2, *The real reason you're so tired*, to be sure that you are doing all you can.

Try another idea...

tiredness, but a study showed that, when iron was given for unexplained tiredness to *non-anaemic* women, their tiredness diminished. Technically this was the placebo response in action, but the researchers concluded that, since many of these non-anaemic women had low iron (just not enough to be clinical), low-grade iron deficiency could still cause symptoms.

Wash down iron-supplying foods with a glass of orange juice: vitamin C helps iron absorption. (Don't take iron supplements without checking with your doctor first.)

Slow, sluggish, everything is in slow motion

Anything else? Feeling cold, depression, weight gain, dry, thickened skin.

Could be? Hypothyroidism.

This is a growing problem and the trouble is not in treatment, but in diagnosis. The symptoms start so slowly that often they are

'I now have no time to be tired.'

Last words of WILHELM I Of
GERMANY, 1888

Defining idea...

misdiagnosed as another disease, for instance, depression or the menopause. If you suspect hypothyroidism, and you're in your forties or fifties, ask your doctor to test your thyroid hormone levels. Replacement hormones can then be prescribed if a deficiency is found. Younger women may have to exclude other diseases before their doctor is willing to test them.

Tired all day despite sleeping at night

Or perhaps you can't sleep at night. On waking, the thought of the day ahead is exhausting.

Anything else? Lack of joy and motivation, anxiety, sleep problems, loss of libido, lack of interest in your life, eating too much or too little.

Could be? Depression.

Exhaustion is one of the prime symptoms of depression. However, depressed people can help themselves by taking a little gentle exercise every day. Exercise has been proven to improve mood and it will help you sleep at night – good because insomnia makes you even more isolated. Your GP can help with anti-depressants and perhaps by offering counselling and other alternatives to drugs. Phonelines such as the Samaritans can listen for free. There is a wealth of advice available now that the stigma associated with depression is disappearing.

Q   My doctor can't find anything wrong. Does that mean I'm fine?

How did it go?

A   *You may have Tired All The Time Syndrome (TATT). Sufferers can usually see clearly how their lifestyle isn't helping their tiredness – they just can't see how to stop it. They might be shift workers, working parents, or prone to depression. In 20–30%, there is no discernible physical problem and up to 50% of cases have a psychological component. Which isn't to say that it's all in your head, but techniques such as cognitive behavioural therapy may help you. The other healer is time. In one study, exhaustion did lift for the majority of the volunteers who described themselves as chronically tired. Those who recovered were markedly more likely to feel that they were generally healthy. The researchers concluded that looking after your emotional wellbeing and improving your general health (so you perceived yourself as a healthy person) were the best indicators that you'd make a recovery.*

Q   Might I have ME?

A   *ME or Chronic Fatigue Syndrome is a complex one. I've interviewed dozens of people – including children – who have ME, and the disease often is triggered by a viral infection. And many times it's not. In these cases, there are strong parallels with burnout – living a life that you've outgrown but driving yourself to succeed at it for whatever reason. That sounds as if I don't take seriously the physical reality of it – but I do. If further reading leads you to suspect ME, just don't discount psychotherapy as one of the routes to getting better.*

49

What are you drinking?

Choosing the right fluids will boost your energy almost instantaneously. Dehydration is a major cause of loss of energy.

But only a lamentable one in ten of us are drinking the 1.5 litres a day of fluid that we should be (and when it's hot, when we exercise and we're ill, that should be two litres).

First, are you drinking enough? Water is the best hydrator of all, mainly because it's got nothing in it that needs to be processed by your body so it supplies the fluid without any stress on your hardworking organs. The simplest way of ensuring that you're drinking enough is to check your urine from mid-morning onwards. It should be straw-coloured.

If you don't drink enough, you get very tired. You may also overeat as we often mistake thirst for hunger. Try drinking a cup of water every hour and you might find your appetite for snacks decreases. You should also find that your need for tea and coffee reduces automatically.

Here's an idea for you... **Want an amazing mid-afternoon pick-up? Take one dessertspoonful of Sea Buckthorn cordial (from health food stores or www. weleda.com) in a cup of boiling water. You might want to add a little honey to begin with until you get used to the taste. Sea Buckthorn has ten times the vitamin C content of lemons (three dessertspoons gives you your daily intake) and vitamin C acts like your usual espresso – it wakes you up. Don't drink it before bedtime or it may keep you awake.**

Which brings us to caffeine. Tea and coffee have the benefit of supplying caffeine, which makes us more alert. Except it doesn't. A recent study has discovered that caffeine doesn't actually work to make us more alert if we drink it regularly. It only has an effect on occasional users. People like me who don't feel they can function without coffee first thing are merely suffering from withdrawal effects. What isn't in dispute (yet) is the effect that caffeine can have on physical performance. Sip an espresso or energy drink half an hour before exercising and you're likely to push harder and achieve more.

Coffee and tea are no longer the 'bogies' they were once thought to be when it comes to hydration. For years we've heard that they are diuretic, causing us to lose fluid. But now that advice has been changed. The water in tea and coffee actually *does* contribute to hydration unless you really overdo it. In summary: the story on caffeine changes every month, but drinking around four cups of ordinary strength coffee or six cups of ordinary strength tea, doesn't appear to do any harm, and may do some good.

My own line is to drink a cup of strong coffee in the morning and then go onto water-based drinks. Caffeine does overwork your adrenal gland which can lead to energy slumps, and too much makes you jittery. Personally, I could drink a lot more than one cup a day and function OK, and so could most people. But if I have more than one cup a day, then I don't get that delicious buzz in the morning from my morning hit.

Vegetable juices are another brilliant hydrator. Go to IDEA 32, *Get in the raw.*

Try another idea...

So for you, me and everyone else, it's a balancing act. Just don't go over the limits set above or you could be robbing your energy bank.

I think it's much easier to get enough good quality fluid if you stop seeing it as a chore and start seeing it as an opportunity. Each glass is its own little ritual, giving your wellbeing and energy levels a fillip. Below is my plan. I stop, I sip, I savour.

THE MAGNIFICENT EIGHT

- *7 a.m.* – Glass of hot water with the juice of a quarter **lemon** on waking – said to aid your liver. Works for me.
- *8 a.m.* – Glass of water to wash down your **multivitamin** and daily fish-oil supplement taken after breakfast.
- *11 a.m.* – A cup of **Rooibus tea**. This red bush tea from South Africa is loaded with antioxidants and its distinctive taste makes it a great substitute for coffee addicts.
- *1 p.m.* – Cup of **green tea** after lunch. It helps rev up your metabolism, and those who drink four cups a day are less likely to suffer from brain ageing.
- *3 p.m.* – Glass of water with an effervescent **vitamin C** tablet – vitamin C wakes you up.
- *5 p.m.* – A glass of **sparkling mineral water cut with fruit juice**. Think of it as a cocktail – the effervescence will get your evening off to a sparkling start.

'Reminds me of my safari in Africa. Somebody forgot the corkscrew and for several days we had to live on nothing but food and water.'

W.C. FIELDS

Defining idea...

- *7 p.m.* – A cup of **mint tea** after dinner – try crushing your own mint leaves in a glass of water or bung in a teabag – either way, great for helping your digestion.
- *9 p.m.* – A cup of **chamomile tea** to soothe you off to sleep.

How did it go?

Q   I'm on the go all day. Are you expecting me to just stop for a cup of fragrant tea when I fancy it?

A   *Carry around a small half-litre bottle of water. Keep it topped up – tap water is fine. Stow it where you can see it – you'll be amazed how often you take a pull. Before every meal, and every time you go to the loo, take some mighty swigs. That should do it.*

Remembering to drink water every time you go to the loo is so easy that even a child can do it – it's how I trained up my kids to get enough water. Incidentally, lack of fluid throughout the day has been found to be a significant contribution to little children's inability to concentrate in class. Think what it's doing to you.

Q   What about energy drinks?

A   *I don't believe in them unless you are just about to exercise, in which case their caffeine content drunk half an hour before exercising should have the same effect as a cup of coffee. Except a cup of coffee is cheaper. My own view is that energy drinks are a clever marketing idea. They give you sugar and caffeine (just like pop) but their health benefits are overplayed. Energy drinks have the same advantages and disadvantages as any other soft drink.*

50

More energy with less sleep

You don't need to sleep for longer to feel more energetic. You just have to sleep smarter.

If sleep is a problem, remember: it's not just quantity that counts, it's quality. Short sleep breaks can have big energy benefits.

Forget the key to the executive washroom. The latest perk in the corporate world is the key to the executive 'snoozepod'. Top businesses and even governments (including the French) are recognising the positive effects on productivity of having a little lie down in the afternoon. The siesta originated because we all have a natural dip in alertness in the early afternoon, even if we don't overdo lunch, and it's especially marked if you've had less sleep the night before. Most of reach for a coffee to counteract the dip, but what experts think we should be doing instead is reaching for an eye mask and grabbing forty winks. A 'powernap' revs up your energy levels for the rest of the day and is worth at least an hour or so of night-time sleep.

The effects could be to do with the very real power of a nap to reduce stress levels. Harvard University found a thirty-minute nap could reduce the risk of burnout, and now we know a nap could save your life – literally. In a study of thousands of

Here's an idea for you... **Keep a torch by the side of your bed if you have to go to the bathroom in the middle of the night. Switching on the light affects melatonin production, which controls sleep and can stop you drifting off again.**

men, it was found that those who napped in the afternoon were 34% less likely to get heart disease. The effects were more pronounced in the men who worked (and had most stress), so researchers think that the beneficial effects of a nap are down to stress reduction. Certainly a nap of just 15–20 minutes allows the body to 'cut off' and cell repair to begin. Your brain has time to disconnect and this allows restorative action to take place. When you wake, you feel more alert, have better concentration and your reactions are quicker. Which is why your boss is likely to be impressed with the effects. Have a nap – get promoted!

Winston Churchill, a world-class napper who worked cabinet meetings around his snoozing schedule, believed a nap wasn't beneficial unless you got undressed and into bed. Not all of us have that luxury. But you can probably find somewhere comfy to put your head down for a short while. Set a timer to go off in 20 minutes' time, close your eyes and relax. If you can't sleep, just resting with your eyes closed is enough to give some benefits.

Remember:

- Nap between 2 p.m. and 4 p.m., the natural energy dip.
- Don't nap later than 6 p.m. or it could affect your sleep later that night.

- A few minutes daily is better than a longer nap once a week. Little and often is what works the magic. Research in Australia discovered that ten-minute mini-naps increased alertness and productivity, but longer than twenty minutes left participants groggy due to 'sleep inertia' – the sluggishness that occurs when a deep sleep is interrupted.

Look at IDEA 6, *How to get enough sleep*, for more on the basics of a good sleep.

Try another idea…

At night, if you have trouble drifting off to sleep, the prime reason is probably anxiety. Read a boring book, eat lettuce sandwiches (lettuce and white bread are sleep-inducing) or keep a pad by your bed to write all your random thoughts down so they're out of your head and on the pad. As a last resort, get up and don't go back to bed until you're already half asleep and absolutely sure that you will drop off. Sometimes lying on the floor or the couch will be enough to allow you to drift off. You may be a sufferer of 'psychophysiological insomnia', which means you can fall asleep but just not in bed. The main thing is to ensure that you don't begin to associate your bed with feelings of frustration. Then you'll never sleep.

NB – Snoring can have the same decibel count as a pneumatic drill, and living with a snorer can start to affect your health within days – or rather nights. Snoring is due to a number of causes. Your doctor can help with advice but persist until the problem is resolved.

'Laugh and the world laughs with you: snore, and you sleep alone.'

ANTHONY BURGESS, author

Defining idea…

223

How did
it go?

Q **I have a five-month-old baby who wakes six times a night. What can I do?**

A *It usually takes a baby around nine months to settle through the night but they can be helped hugely to sleep better, waking only once, say, from a few months. There is wealth of good advice on settling babies into a routine once they're a few months old and it really is worth seeking out what works for you. A few boundaries around sleep don't make you a bad parent; sleep deprivation might. One idea: a three-sided cot that can be propped up next to your bed, so at least you don't have to get out of bed to feed or comfort him.*

Q **I wake up during the night. Why?**

A *Look to the light. Streets are much brighter than they used to be and if you don't have blackout blinds or curtains, it might be worth fitting them. Ban computers, TVs and digital clocks – even a little light impacts on your retina when your lids are closed. Replace lumpy mattresses, pillows and duvets. Banish clutter. Harvard Medical School believes that crap lying around your bed is what's known as a 'stimulus trigger', preventing your mind from switching off. Finally, if you have a pet, keep it out of the room. Researchers at the Mayo Clinic in the US found that 53% of people who let pets sleep on their bed have disturbed sleep every night.*

51

Makeover your metabolism

Want to have more energy *and* lose weight? Yes? Then read on.

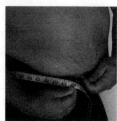

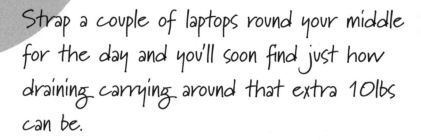

Strap a couple of laptops round your middle for the day and you'll soon find just how draining carrying around that extra 10lbs can be.

If you're overweight, losing a few pounds will help your energy levels. But how do you do it without feeling more drained? Try this; it's called calorie cycling. Versions of it have been around for years, but for some reason it isn't trumpeted by the slimming industry. Maybe because it works.

The reason I like it is that it is realistic. It takes into account that none of us can stick to a diet all the time. Of course, some people do spend their lives on a diet – stick-thin celebs are the most visible example. But if they ever slip up, they will balloon overnight because constant starvation has lowered their metabolic rate – the rate at which they burn off calories – to that of a vole.

Which brings us back to calorie cycling, because it works on the principle that by mixing up your calorie count, your metabolic rate stays on its toes, so to speak. Your metabolic rate doesn't drop as you lose weight; in fact, it revs up. It's thought that

Here's an idea for you... **Stock up on flaxseed oil, the darling of dieting gurus. This oil apparently activates leptin – the hormone that boosts metabolism. Drizzle it on porridge, salad or vegetables, or swallow a couple of spoonfuls neat. Healthy oils curb cravings, too.**

dieting suppresses production of an appetite-regulating hormone, leptin. High leptin production means a high metabolism; reduced leptin means metabolism goes down and your appetite goes up. This mechanism helped our Stone Age ancestors cope with famine. Now it just makes us fat.

How does calorie cycling work? Simple. You diet for a few days, then for one day you eat pretty much what you like. There is evidence that it works. Research done by the National Institute of Health in the States discovered that when healthy young men restricted calories and then binged, their metabolism rose by 9% on the morning after their binge day. It's thought binge days 'reset' leptin production. Below are some ideas. For more sophisticated diet plans and more advice read *The Rotation Diet*, *The Warrior Diet*, *Eating for Life* and *The Abs Diet*. (Don't follow *any* diet without your doctor's advice if you have a medical condition or suspect you could have one.)

THE HARD-CORE VERSION

This version means you eat lightly during the day (but frequently), and more at night. You further mix things up by dropping most carbs for a couple of days, then adding them back in. The advantage is that you are never more than three days away from a pudding.

Eat unlimited amounts of fruit and salad during the day, with eggs as your only protein. (I strongly advise having a boiled egg for breakfast or, if you're like me, you'll keel over.) At night, eat unlimited amounts of vegetables with a large-ish palm-sized piece of protein – beef, chicken turkey, fish, or tofu. Don't eat any starch or sugars.

Combine this with IDEA 42, *Supermarket savvy*, for maximum energy boosting.

Try another idea...

Follow this for two days, then switch to one day of eating much the same but, after you've eaten your evening meal, have some carbohydrates – a roll, a baked potato, some pasta or rice and a dessert, too, if you like. You must eat the protein and vegetables first because the theory goes that you should never eat starchy carbohydrate foods on an empty stomach. The sugars are rapidly absorbed into your bloodstream resulting in a blood-sugar spike and release of insulin, which encourages your body to store excess energy as fat. Eating non-starchy carbs such as vegetables, and protein beforehand slows down the absorption of sugars.

THE STRAIGHTFORWARD VERSION

Eat around 1700 calories for four or five days. Eat around 2000 calories for one day. Eat 1700 calories for four or five days. Eat around 2000 calories for one day. You get the picture. Don't do this for more than a month – it's low in calories.

Typical 1700 calories

- Breakfast – bowl of cereal with semi-skimmed milk and a small glass of orange juice
- Mid-morning – half a dozen almonds
- Lunch – sandwich, apple
- Mid-afternoon – orange
- Dinner – plate of chicken and vegetable stir-fry followed by a peach and a small glass of wine.

'The doctor of the future will give no medicine but will interest his or her patients in the care of the human frame, a proper diet and the cause and prevention of disease.'
THOMAS EDISON

Defining idea...

Q   Bit complicated for me. Isn't there something simpler?

A   *Yes, I know what you mean. I'm not mad on becoming obsessed with food either. Try this. Stick to a low-calorie, low-carb or low-fat diet of your choice for six days and eat what you like on the seventh. You'll find that you'll go mad on the 'free day' for a few weeks but then, if you are keeping to it during the week, when the novelty wears off, you don't want to eat too much on the seventh day.*

I've read all sorts of different versions of the same principle, for instance, following a diet for three weeks, then one week off (hardest of all I think – after a week off I'd carry on staying off forever). But it might work for you.

Q   Would you get results if you ate normally for two days and dieted for one day?

A   *No. Two days off, one day on a low-calorie regime, is what body builders do to put on weight. The big danger of calorie cycling is that you 'slide' and have more days off than on. If on those days off you eat what you like, you'll end up gaining weight. As a rule of thumb, never have two days off in a row. Some versions of calorie cycling offer plans of how to do it but, in my opinion, if you come off a diet for two days, you'll never go back on it again. This whole idea is no good if you can't trust yourself to come off a diet for one day and then go back on it.*

If you do only one thing ...

Choose one of these short, sharp, quick-acting methods of feeling more energetic pronto.

These will perk you up by suppertime.

TWO WAYS TO ENERGISE YOUR IMAGE

- *Be kind.* If you enjoy a good gossip, take note of the research from Ohio State University that shows that in 55% of cases, if you talk about the negative personality trait of someone else, the listener associates the negative characteristics not with them, but with you. On the other hand, if you say someone has got a great new job or is looking brilliant, the listener judges you to be successful or more attractive.
- *Sit down carefully.* When entering a room, choose a seat facing the door with your back to the wall. This is the 'power seat'. Sitting here makes you feel secure and you'll find people naturally defer to you and treat you with more respect.

FOUR PRODUCTS TO CARRY IN YOUR HANDBAG ...

- *Gelsemium 30C* – a homeopathic remedy that helps concentration and boosts your mental energy.
- *Valerian* – in one trial, 44% of insomniacs reported sleeping well after taking valerian and 89% reported an improved sleep.

- *Olive Bach Flower Remedy* – it can help if you are exhausted physically and mentally. Use it when you are absolutely running on empty: it gives you back your zest for life and restores vitality.
- *Peppermint chewing gum* – Harvard research shows lemon and peppermint wake you up. Chewing peppermint gum has a double whammy effect – the muscle action helps alertness even when the rest of your body is motionless.

... AND ONE THING TO LEAVE AT HOME

- *Your bills* – research shows popping bills in your bag to pay later subtly stresses you out all day and drains energy. (But leaving bills lying around does the same thing – file them or deal with them immediately.)

FIVE WAYS TO ENERGISE YOUR WORK LIFE

- *Ignore the view of the car park.* Exposure to a 'natural scene' is an excellent antidote to mental fatigue. Get to the park if you can at lunch or pin up some beautiful pictures of green countryside above your desk.
- *Remember the 90:120 rule.* Plan your working day in 120-minute blocks. US research shows that somewhere between 90 and 120 minutes we lose focus. After 90 minutes, stop, take a few minutes to walk around, stretch, drink a glass or water or have a cup of tea. When you return to work do another sort of task until the 120-minute mark – email, make calls or switch to another job. After two hours, plan what to do for the next 120-

Here's an idea for you...

Best supper for a good night's sleep: pasta with homemade pesto sauce. Basil in the pesto is a powerful sedative; the carbs in pasta will send you to sleep. Finish with hot milk sprinkled with cinnamon (the milk will help you sleep) or a chamomile tea.

minute block. You'll find that you have more momentum and are more productive.

IDEA 15, *Avoid the brain drain,*has other quick ways of combating mental energy slump.

Try another idea...

- *Open mail standing next to waste paper bin* – and throw out rubbish then and there.
- *Keep a notebook with you* – and write down every potential task as it pops into your brain – this brings home to you that you almost certainly can't do it all. You have to pick and choose.
- *Don't screen calls* – you only have to call people back later. But if you have to screen, set aside a slot at the end of the day to make calls. A bad conscience is an energy drain.

FOUR BEDTIME HABITS THAT BOOST ENERGY NEXT DAY

- *Don't exercise* in the three hours before you go to bed. But a study shows that people who do exercise for at least half an hour, four times a week, fall asleep 12 minutes earlier and sleeep for 42 minutes longer than people who do no exercise at all.
- *Schedule laughs.* Invest in the DVD set of your favourite comedy and watch a few minutes every evening. Humour arouses and distracts the mind from its usual patterns and makes you more relaxed and energised.
- *Have an Epsom salts bath.* Dissolve 500g or so of Epsom salts (from any chemist) in warm water and relax for thirty minutes. Sip water throughout. Avoid if you have high blood pressure, heart trouble or diabetes. Go straight to bed afterwards.
- *Get to bed by 9.30.* Even if you can't sleep, listen to the radio, soothing music, books on tape, or read. Resting your body helps restore your energy.

'Every time you don't listen to your inner guidance, you feel a loss of energy, a loss of power, a sense of spiritual deadness.'

SHAKTI GAWAIN, guru and author

Defining idea...

How did it go?

Q I've tried the power seat and I can't believe it, but it worked. Anything else like that?

A *I came across the power seat theory when the Chinese theory of energy placement, feng shui, was fashionable. Crazy but I've found that the experts' advice on the energy levels generated by the number of guests at a party to be spookily accurate. Two is great for people in the 'honeymoon' phase, who still want to bond. But if you've been friends for ages, just the two of you can be stagnant. New blood will ensure that you don't take each other for granted. Three is a fun number. The energy is constantly shifting. Four is solid and makes for good communication. Friends who meet at a dinner for four can become the closest friends. Five is a risk – it's slightly unstable, which can be great or disastrous. Six starts well, relaxed and animated, but often peters out. Seven is serious – conversation may get onto spiritual subjects and it's great for making money – get seven round the table to discuss a business venture. Eight is a lot of energy but it is double four and makes for a great night. The energy is grounded and steady – good for a larger dinner party.*

Q The Bach flower remedy was handy. Any others?

A *Most chemists stock the whole range and you can use different remedies to suit your problems. Olive is for when you are running on empty. If your exhaustion is different – you're weary, mentally rather than physically tired – you might find Hornbeam is better for you. It's perfect for that 'Monday morning' feeling.*

The end...

Or is it a new beginning?

We hope that these ideas will have inspired you to try new things to get you bursting with energy. We hope you've found that making small but effective lifestyle changes has worked and that you're already starting the day with a nutritious breakfast, taking a bit more exercise and have had a go at zapping those black holes. You should be well on your way to a bright and bouncy new you.

So why not let us know about it? Tell us how you got on. What did it for you – what really put a spring in your step? Maybe you've got some tips of your own that you'd like to share. If you liked this you may find we have more brilliant ideas for other areas that could help change your life for the better. You'll find us, and a host of other brilliant ideas, online at www.infideas.com.

Or if you prefer to write, then send your letters to:
Boundless Energy
The Infinite Ideas Company Ltd
36 St Giles, Oxford, OX1 3LD, United Kingdom

We want to know what you think, because we're all working on making our lives better too. Give us your feedback and you could win a copy of another 52 *Brilliant Ideas* book of your choice. Or maybe get a crack at writing your own.

Good luck. Be brilliant.

Offer one

CASH IN YOUR IDEAS

We hope you enjoy this book. We hope it inspires, amuses, educates and entertains you. But we don't assume that you're a novice, or that this is the first book that you've bought on the subject. You've got ideas of your own. Maybe our author has missed an idea that you use successfully. If so, why not put it in an email and send it to: yourauthormissedatrick@infideas.com, and if we like it we'll post it on our bulletin board. Better still, if your idea makes it into print we'll send you four books of your choice or the cash equivalent. You'll be fully credited so that everyone knows you've had another Brilliant Idea.

Offer two

HOW COULD YOU REFUSE?

Amazing discounts on bulk quantities of Infinite Ideas books are available to corporations, professional associations and other organisations.

For details call us on:
+44 (0)1865 514888
fax: +44 (0)1865 514777
or e-mail: info@infideas.com

Where it's at ...

Boundless energy: *52 brilliant ideas for recapturing your bounce* is part of the acclaimed **52 Brilliant Ideas** series. If you found this book helpful, you may want to take advantage of this special offer exclusive to all readers of *Boundless energy*. Choose any two books from the selection below and you'll get one of them free of charge*. See overleaf for prices and details on how to place your order.

brilliant ideas

Stress proof your life
52 brilliant ideas for taking control
By Elisabeth Wilson

Stop smoking
52 brilliant ideas to kick the habit for good
By Peter Cross and Clive Hopwood

Healthy cooking for children
52 brilliant ideas to dump the junk
By Mandy Francis

Control your blood pressure
52 brilliant ideas for keeping a lid on hypertension
By Dr Rob Hicks

Downshift to the good life
Scale it down and live it up
By Lynn Huggins-Cooper

Inspired creative writing
NEW EDITION
Secrets of the master wordsmiths
By Alexander Gordon Smith

Healthy heart
Keep your heart happy
By Dr Ruth Chambers

Win at the gym
Secrets of fitness and health success
By Steve Shipside

Get healthy for good
52 brilliant ideas for mind and body well-being
By Kate Cook

Transform your life
52 brilliant ideas for becoming the person you want to be
By Penny Ferguson

For more detailed information on these books and others published by Infinite Ideas please visit www.infideas.com

* Postage at £2.75 per delivery address is additional.

Choose any two titles from below and receive one free

Qty	Title	RRP
	Stress proof your life	£12.99
	Stop smoking	£12.99
	Healthy cooking for children	£12.99
	Control your blood pressure	£12.99
	Downshift to the good life	£12.99
	Inspired creative writing	£12.99
	Healthy heart	£12.99
	Win at the gym	£12.99
	Get healthy for good	£12.99
	Transform your life	£12.99

Subtract lowest priced book if ordering two titles	
Add £2.75 postage per delivery address	
Final TOTAL	

Name: ....

Delivery address: ....

....

....

....

E-mail:...Tel (in case of problems): ....

By post Fill in all relevant details, cut out or photocopy this page and send along with a cheque made payable to Infinite Ideas. Send to: *Boundless energy* Offer, Infinite Ideas, 36 St Giles, Oxford OX1 3LD, UK.

Credit card orders over the telephone Call +44 (0) 1865 514 888. Lines are open 9am to 5pm Monday to Friday. Just mention the promotion code 'BEAD07.'

Please note that no payment will be processed until your order has been dispatched. Goods are dispatched through Royal Mail within 14 working days, when in stock. We never forward personal details on to third parties or bombard you with junk mail. This offer is valid for UK and RoI residents only until 31 July 2008. Any questions or comments please contact us on 01865 514 888 or email info@infideas.com.

Start re-energising with this offer from Champneys

CHAMPNEYS
HEALTH RESORTS

Start as you mean to go on with this energy-boosting offer. Pamper yourself at **Champneys** and enjoy a **15% discount** on any standard booking. You'll soon be on your way to feeling revitalised and recapturing your bounce.

Champneys provides a range of premier health resorts across the United Kingdom, all offering exceptional standards in beauty, fitness, nutrition and holistic health. Every resort is designed to be a haven from the stresses of everyday life. They are perfect to visit on your own, with friends or as a couple. Choose from the original Champneys Tring in Hertfordshire, the modern Springs in Leicestershire, the enchanting Forest Mere in Hampshire or the cosy Henlow in Bedfordshire. For more information visit **www.champneys.com.**

To take advantage of this special offer please ring Champneys directly on 08703 300 300 and quote 'Boundless energy' when making your booking.

Terms & conditions
This offer is valid until 31st December 2008 and is subject to availability. This offer cannot be used in conjunction with any other offer or promotion and applies to new reservations only. The offer cannot be applied on or during bank holidays.